COMMON CORE

MATH

Activities that Captivate, Motivate, and Reinforce

Grade 6

by Marjorie Frank

IncentivePublications

BY WORLD BOOK
a Scott Fetzer company

Illustrated by Kathleen Bullock
Cover by Penny Laporte

Print Edition ISBN 978-1-62950-235-9
E-book Edition ISBN 978-1-62950-236-6 (PDF)

World Book, Inc.
233 North Michigan Avenue
Suite 2000
Chicago, Illinois, 60601 U.S.A.

For information about World Book and Incentive Publications products, call **1-800-967-5325,** or visit our websites at **www.worldbook.com** and **www.incentivepublications.com.**

Printed in the United States of America by Sheridan Books, Inc.
Chelsea, Michigan
1st Printing July 2014

CONTENTS

The Number System

Expressions and Equations

Statistics and Probability

Assessment and Answer Keys

Great Support for Common Core State Standards!

Invite your students to join in on mysteries and adventures with colorful characters! They will delight in the high-appeal topics and engaging visuals. They can

　　. . . tackle statistics with a building-climbing "human spider";

　　. . . commiserate with campers outnumbered by mosquitoes and bears;

　　. . . solve real-life problems about racing garbage cans and baby carriages;

　　. . . juggle data about roller coaster-riding marathons;

　　. . . drop in on extreme eating contests;

　　. . . consider such unusual sports as sword swallowing and cricket spitting;

　　. . . figure out how much hot surface a fire-walker must endure;

　　. . . calculate rates of broken bones in a rodeo;

　　. . . graph sprained ankles, bloody noses, and other sports injuries;

　　. . . meet some folks who set such strange records as skipping rope while brushing their teeth;

　　. . . and tackle many other delightful tasks.

And while they engage in these adventures, they will be moving toward competence in critical math skills that they need for success in the real world.

How to Use This Book

- The pages are tools to support your teaching of the concepts, processes, and skills outlined in the Common Core State Standards. This is not a curriculum; it is a collection of engaging experiences for you to use as you do math with your students or children.

- Use any given page to introduce, explain, teach, practice, extend, assess, provide independent work, start a discussion about, or get students collaborating on a skill or concept.

- Use any page in a large-group or small-group setting to deepen understandings and expand knowledge or standards and skills.

- Pages are not intended for use solely as independent work. Do the activities together or review and discuss the work together.

- Each activity is focused on a particular standard, but most make use of or can be expanded to strengthen other standards as well.

- The book is organized according to the Common Core math domains. Use the tables on pages 9 to 16, the page labels, and notations on the Contents pages to identify the standards supported by each page.

- For further mastery of Common Core State Standards for Mathematics, use the suggestions on page 8.

About Common Core State Standards for Mathematics

The Common Core State Standards for Mathematics at the middle-grades level aim to expand conceptual understanding of the key ideas of math while they strengthen foundational skills, operations, and principles. They identify what students should know, understand, and be able to do—with an emphasis on explaining principles and applying them to a wide range of situations. To best help students achieve these robust standards for math . . .

1. Know the standards well. Keep them in front of you. Understand for yourself the big picture of what the standards seek to do. (See www.corestandards.org.)

2. Work to apply, expand, and deepen student skills. With activities in this book (or any learning activities), plan to include
   . . . interaction with peers in pairs, small groups, and large groups
   . . . plenty of discussion, integration, and hands-on work with math concepts
   . . . questioning, analyzing, modeling math situations, explaining what you are doing and thinking, using tools effectively, and applying to real world problems
   . . . lots of observation, meaningful feedback, follow-up, and reflection

3. Ask questions that advance reasoning, application, and real-life connection:
   - *What, exactly, IS the problem?*
   - *Can you solve this another way?*
   - *Does this make sense? (Why or why not?)*
   - *Can you state the problem in a different way?*
   - *What information is needed to solve this problem?*
   - *What information in the problem is not needed?*
   - *What operations do you need to use?*
   - *If we change ___, what will happen to ___?*
   - *What tools do you need to solve this?*
   - *Can you illustrate your problem-solving process?*
   - *What did you learn from solving this problem?*
   - *When could you use this? Where could you use this?*
   - *How did you arrive at your answer?*
   - *How can you show that your answer is right?*
   - *Where else have you seen a problem like this?*
   - *What does this ask you to do?*
   - *What led you to this conclusion?*
   - *How could we figure this out?*
   - *What was the first step you took?*
   - *How could you make a model of this?*
   - *How could you demonstrate your solution?*
   - *If ___ changed, how would the solution change?*
   - *What patterns do you notice?*
   - *Where have you seen this in real life?*
   - *What does this remind you of?*
   - *Could there be another answer?*
   - *How could you show this a different way?*
   - *If this is true, what else might be true?*
   - *How can you explain your answer?*
   - *How could you ask that question differently?*
   - *What will you do next?*

Standards for Mathematical Practice, Grades K-12

Math Practice Standard	Standard	Pages that Support
MP1	Make sense of problems and persevere in solving them.	18-34, 36-60, 62-88, 90-106, 108-126
MP2	Reason abstractly and quantitatively.	18-34, 36-60, 62-88, 90-106, 108-126
MP3	Construct viable arguments and critique the reasoning of others.	22, 23, 24, 33, 36-37, 43, 47, 48-49, 64, 75, 76, 78, 106, 108, 109, 111, 114, 115, 117, 119, 120, 122, 124-125, 126
MP4	Model with mathematics.	18-34, 36-60, 62-88, 90-106, 108-126
MP5	Use appropriate tools strategically.	18-34, 36-60, 62-88, 90-106, 108-126
MP6	Attend to precision.	18-34, 36-60, 62-88, 90-106, 108-126
MP7	Look for and make use of structure.	18-34, 36-60, 62-88, 90-106, 108-126
MP8	Look for and express regularity in repeated reasoning.	18-34, 62-88, 108-126

Grade 6 Common Core State Standards for Mathematical Content

6.RP.A   Ratios and Proportional Relationships

Math Content Standard	Standard	Pages that Support
	**Understand ratio concepts and use ratio reasoning to solve problems.**	
6.RP.A.1	Understand the concept of a ratio and use ratio language to describe a ratio relationship between two quantities. *For example, "The ratio of wings to beaks in the bird house at the zoo was 2:1, because for every 2 wings there was 1 beak." "For every vote candidate A received, candidate C received nearly three votes."*	18-19, 20, 21, 22, 23, 24-25, 26-27, 28, 29, 30, 31, 32, 33
6.RP.A.2	Understand the concept of a unit rate a/b associated with a ratio a:b with b ≠ 0, and use rate language in the context of a ratio relationship. *For example, "This recipe has a ratio of 3 cups of flour to 4 cups of sugar, so there is $\frac{3}{4}$ cup of flour for each cup of sugar." "We paid $75 for 15 hamburgers, which is a rate of $5 per hamburger."*	22, 23, 26-27, 28
6.RP.A.3	Use ratio and rate reasoning to solve real-world and mathematical problems, e.g., by reasoning about tables of equivalent ratios, tape diagrams, double number line diagrams, or equations.	18-19, 20, 21, 22, 23, 24-25, 26-27, 28, 29, 30, 31, 32, 33, 34
6.RP.A.3a	Make tables of equivalent ratios relating quantities with whole-number measurements, find missing values in the tables, and plot the pairs of values on the coordinate plane. Use tables to compare ratios.	22, 23, 24-25
6.RP.A.3b	Solve unit rate problems including those involving unit pricing and constant speed. For example, if it took 7 hours to mow 4 lawns, then at that rate, how many lawns could be mowed in 35 hours? At what rate were lawns being mowed?	20, 21, 26-27, 28
6.RP.A.3c	Find a percent of a quantity as a rate per 100 (e.g., 30% of a quantity means $\frac{30}{100}$ times the quantity); solve problems involving finding the whole, given a part and the percent.	29, 30, 31, 32
6.RP.A.3d	Use ratio reasoning to convert measurement units; manipulate and transform units appropriately when multiplying or dividing quantities.	33-34

10

Grade 6 Common Core State Standards for Mathematical Content

6.NS The Number System

Math Content Standard	Standard	Pages that Support
Apply and extend previous understandings of multiplication and division to divide fractions by fractions.		
6.NS.A.1	Interpret and compute quotients of fractions, and solve word problems involving division of fractions by fractions, e.g., by using visual fraction models and equations to represent the problem. *For example, create a story context for $(\frac{2}{3}) \div (\frac{3}{4})$ and use a visual fraction model to show the quotient; use the relationship between multiplication and division to explain that $(\frac{2}{3}) \div (\frac{3}{4}) = \frac{8}{9}$ because $\frac{3}{4}$ of $\frac{8}{9}$ is $\frac{2}{3}$. (In general, $(\frac{a}{b}) \div (\frac{c}{d}) = \frac{ad}{bc}$.) How much chocolate will each person get if 3 people share $\frac{1}{2}$ lb of chocolate equally? How many $\frac{3}{4}$-cup servings are in $\frac{2}{3}$ of a cup of yogurt? How wide is a rectangular strip of land with length $\frac{3}{4}$ mi and area $\frac{1}{2}$ square mi?*	36-37
Compute fluently with multi-digit numbers and find common factors and multiples.		
6.NS.B.2	Fluently divide multi-digit numbers using the standard algorithm.	38, 39, 40
6.NS.B.3	Use ratio and rate reasoning to solve real-world and mathematical problems, e.g., by reasoning about tables of equivalent ratios, tape diagrams, double number line diagrams, or equations.	18-19, 20, 21, 22, 23, 24-25, 26-27, 28, 29, 30, 31, 32, 33, 34
6.NS.B.4	Find the greatest common factor of two whole numbers less than or equal to 100 and the least common multiple of two whole numbers less than or equal to 12. Use the distributive property to express a sum of two whole numbers 1–100 with a common factor as a multiple of a sum of two whole numbers with no common factor. For example, express 36 + 8 as 4 (9 + 2).	42, 43, 44
Apply and extend previous understandings of numbers to the system of rational numbers.		
6.NS.C.5	Understand that positive and negative numbers are used together to describe quantities having opposite directions or values (e.g., temperature above/below zero, elevation above/below sea level, credits/debits, positive/negative electric charge); use positive and negative numbers to represent quantities in real-world contexts, explaining the meaning of 0 in each situation.	45, 46, 47, 48-49, 50, 51, 52, 53, 54, 55, 56, 57, 58-59, 60

The Number System standards continue on the next page.

Grade 6 Common Core State Standards for Mathematical Content

6.NS   The Number System, continued

Math Content Standard	Standard	Pages that Support
	Apply and extend previous understandings of numbers to the system of rational numbers.	
6.NS.C.6	Understand a rational number as a point on the number line. Extend number line diagrams and coordinate axes familiar from previous grades to represent points on the line and in the plane with negative number coordinates.	47-51
6.NS.C.6a	Recognize opposite signs of numbers as indicating locations on opposite sides of 0 on the number line; recognize that the opposite of the opposite of a number is the number itself, e.g., –(–3) = 3, and that 0 is its own opposite.	47
6.NS.C.6b	Understand signs of numbers in ordered pairs as indicating locations in quadrants of the coordinate plane; recognize that when two ordered pairs differ only by signs, the locations of the points are related by reflections across one or both axes.	48-49, 57, 58-59, 60
6.NS.C.6c	Find and position integers and other rational numbers on a horizontal or vertical number line diagram; find and position pairs of integers and other rational numbers on a coordinate plane.	48-49, 50, 51, 52, 53, 57, 58-59, 60
6.NS.C.7	Understand ordering and absolute value of rational numbers.	52-60
6.NS.C.7a	Interpret statements of inequality as statements about the relative position of two numbers on a number line diagram. For example, interpret –3 > –7 as a statement that –3 is located to the right of –7 on a number line oriented from left to right.	52
6.NS.C.7b	Write, interpret, and explain statements of order for rational numbers in real-world contexts. For example, write –3 °C > –7 °C to express the fact that –3 °C is warmer than –7 °C.	53-54
6.NS.C.7c	Understand the absolute value of a rational number as its distance from 0 on the number line; interpret absolute value as magnitude for a positive or negative quantity in a real-world situation. For example, for an account balance of –30 dollars, write |–30| = 30 to describe the size of the debt in dollars.	55, 56
6.NS.C.7d	Distinguish comparisons of absolute value from statements about order. For example, recognize that an account balance less than –30 dollars represents a debt greater than 30 dollars.	56
6.NS.C.8	Solve real-world and mathematical problems by graphing points in all four quadrants of the coordinate plane. Include use of coordinates and absolute value to find distances between points with the same first coordinate or the same second coordinate.	57, 58-59, 60

Grade 6 Common Core State Standards for Mathematical Content

6.EE   Expressions and Equations

Math Content Standard	Standard	Pages that Support
Apply and extend previous understandings of arithmetic to algebraic expressions.		
6.EE.A.1	Write and evaluate numerical expressions involving whole-number exponents.	62, 63
6.EE.A.2	Write, read, and evaluate expressions in which letters stand for numbers.	64-73
6.EE.A.2a	Write expressions that record operations with numbers and with letters standing for numbers. For example, express the calculation "Subtract y from 5" as 5 – y.	64, 65, 70, 73
6.EE.A.2b	Identify parts of an expression using mathematical terms (sum, term, product, factor, quotient, coefficient); view one or more parts of an expression as a single entity. *For example, describe the expression 2 (8 + 7) as a product of two factors; view (8 + 7) as both a single entity and a sum of two terms.*	66, 67
6.EE.A.2c	Evaluate expressions at specific values of their variables. Include expressions that arise from formulas used in real-world problems. Perform arithmetic operations, including those involving whole-number exponents, in the conventional order when there are no parentheses to specify a particular order (Order of Operations). *For example, use the formulas V = s3 and A = 6 s² to find the volume and surface area of a cube with sides of length s = $\frac{1}{2}$.*	68, 69, 70, 72
6.EE.A.3	Apply the properties of operations to generate equivalent expressions. *For example, apply the distributive property to the expression 3 (2 + x) to produce the equivalent expression 6 + 3x; apply the distributive property to the expression 24x + 18y to produce the equivalent expression 6 (4x + 3y); apply properties of operations to y + y + y to produce the equivalent expression 3y.*	70, 71, 72, 73
6.EE.A.4	Identify when two expressions are equivalent (i.e., when the two expressions name the same number regardless of which value is substituted into them). *For example, the expressions y + y + y and 3y are equivalent because they name the same number regardless of which number y stands for.*	73

Expressions and Equations standards continue on the next page.

Grade 6 Common Core State Standards for Mathematical Content

6.EE   Expressions and Equations, continued

Math Content Standard	Standard	Pages that Support
	Reason about and solve one-variable equations and inequalities.	
6.EE.B.5	Understand solving an equation or inequality as a process of answering a question: which values from a specified set, if any, make the equation or inequality true? Use substitution to determine whether a given number in a specified set makes an equation or inequality true.	74, 75, 76, 77, 78, 79, 80, 81, 82, 83, 84, 85, 86-87, 88
6.EE.B.6	Use variables to represent numbers and write expressions when solving a real-world or mathematical problem; understand that a variable can represent an unknown number, or, depending on the purpose at hand, any number in a specified set.	76, 77, 78
6.EE.B.7	Solve real-world and mathematical problems by writing and solving equations of the form $x + p = q$ and $px = q$ for cases in which p, q and x are all nonnegative rational numbers.	79, 80, 81, 82
6.EE.B.8	Write an inequality of the form $x > c$ or $x < c$ to represent a constraint or condition in a real-world or mathematical problem. Recognize that inequalities of the form $x > c$ or $x < c$ have infinitely many solutions; represent solutions of such inequalities on number line diagrams.	83, 84
	Represent and analyze quantitative relationships between dependent and independent variables.	
	Use variables to represent two quantities in a real-world problem that change in relationship to one another; write an equation to express one quantity, thought of as the dependent variable, in terms of the other quantity, thought of as the independent variable. Analyze the relationship between the dependent and independent variables using graphs and tables, and relate these to the equation. *For example, in a problem involving motion at constant speed, list and graph ordered pairs of distances and times, and write the equation $d = 65t$ to represent the relationship between distance and time.*	85, 86-87, 88

Grade 6 Common Core State Standards for Mathematical Content

6.G   Geometry

Math Content Standard	Standard	Pages that Support
Solve real-world and mathematical problems involving area, surface area, and volume.		
6.G.A.1	Find the area of right triangles, other triangles, special quadrilaterals, and polygons by composing into rectangles or decomposing into triangles and other shapes; apply these techniques in the context of solving real-world and mathematical problems.	90, 91, 92-93, 94
6.G.A.2	Find the volume of a right rectangular prism with fractional edge lengths by packing it with unit cubes of the appropriate unit fraction edge lengths, and show that the volume is the same as would be found by multiplying the edge lengths of the prism. Apply the formulas $V = l\,w\,h$ and $V = b\,h$ to find volumes of right rectangular prisms with fractional edge lengths in the context of solving real-world and mathematical problems.	95, 96, 97, 98-99
6.G.A.3	Draw polygons in the coordinate plane given coordinates for the vertices; use coordinates to find the length of a side joining points with the same first coordinate or the same second coordinate. Apply these techniques in the context of solving real-world and mathematical problems.	100-101, 102-103
6.G.A.4	Represent three-dimensional figures using nets made up of rectangles and triangles, and use the nets to find the surface area of these figures. Apply these techniques in the context of solving real-world and mathematical problems.	104-105, 106

Grade 6 Common Core State Standards for Mathematical Content

6.SP   Statistics and Probability

Math Content Standard	Standard	Pages that Support
Develop understanding of statistical variability.		
6.SP.A.1	Recognize a statistical question as one that anticipates variability in the data related to the question and accounts for it in the answers. *For example, "How old am I?" is not a statistical question, but "How old are the students in my school?" is a statistical question because one anticipates variability in students' ages.*	108, 109
6.SP.A.2	Understand that a set of data collected to answer a statistical question has a distribution which can be described by its center, spread, and overall shape.	110, 111
6.SP.A.3	Recognize that a measure of center for a numerical data set summarizes all of its values with a single number, while a measure of variation describes how its values vary with a single number.	112, 113, 124-125, 126
Summarize and describe distributions.		
6.SP.B.4	Display numerical data in plots on a number line, including dot plots, histograms, and box plots.	114, 115, 116, 117, 118, 119, 120
6.SP.B.5	Summarize numerical data sets in relation to their context, such as by:	121-126
6.SP.B.5a	Reporting the number of observations.	121
6.SP.B.5b	Describing the nature of the attribute under investigation, including how it was measured and its units of measurement.	122, 123
6.SP.B.5c	Giving quantitative measures of center (median and/or mean) and variability (interquartile range and/or mean absolute deviation), as well as describing any overall pattern and any striking deviations from the overall pattern with reference to the context in which the data were gathered.	124-125
6.SP.B.5d	Relating the choice of measures of center and variability to the shape of the data distribution and the context in which the data were gathered.	126

RATIOS
AND
PROPORTIONAL
RELATIONSHIPS

Grade 6

There's a high ratio of complaints to steps.

INTRUDER ALERT

A **ratio** is a comparison between two numbers or amounts. Ratios are used to compare all kinds of things, such as ages, prices, weights, times, or distances.

Help! There are 12 spiders, 5 mosquitos, and 6 rats in my tent!

What is the ratio of spiders to rats? You can write the ratio in three ways:

. . . as a fraction: $\frac{12}{6}$ . . . with a colon: 12:6   . . . with the word *to*: 12 *to* 6

Answer these ratio questions about the intruders into this tent.

1. What is the ratio of mosquitoes to spiders in the tent? (Circle one.)

 12 to 5   12:17 $\frac{12}{5}$ 5 to 12

2. What is the ratio of rats to mosquitoes in the tent?

3. What is the ratio of rats to the total number of creatures in the tent (including the boy)?

4. What is the ratio in #3 (above) reduced to lowest terms?

5. What is the **reduced ratio** of spiders to rats?

6. The boy has 30 mosquito bites. What is the reduced ratio of bites to mosquitoes?

Fortunately, the ratio of cats to rats is 0 to 6.

Name _____

Use with page 19.

Circle the ratio that answers each question.

7. 11 rats ate equal amounts of chocolate from campers' backpacks. They ate a total of 121 ounces of chocolate. What is the reduced ratio of chocolate to rats?

$\frac{1}{11}$ $\frac{11}{1}$ $\frac{121}{132}$ $\frac{21}{11}$

8. On this camping trip, Chad identified 12 of the 84 spiders he saw. What is the reduced ratio of the spiders he identified to those he did not?

$\frac{12}{106}$ $\frac{12}{94}$ $\frac{1}{7}$ $\frac{7}{1}$

9. The campers had visits from bears 3 of the 4 nights they camped. What is the ratio of the nights there were no visits to the total number of nights they camped?

$\frac{3}{4}$ $\frac{1}{4}$ $\frac{4}{7}$ $\frac{1}{3}$

10. On one night, a group of 9 rats carried away 45 kg of food. What is the reduced ratio of rats to food weight?

$\frac{5}{1}$ $\frac{1}{5}$ 9:45 $\frac{45}{9}$

11. On the first night, there were 60 mosquitoes spread out evenly among 4 tents. What is the ratio of tents to mosquitoes?

1 to 15   4 to 64   4 to 1   1 to 4

12. When the campers hit the trail the second day, 54 spiders came along for the trip inside nine backpacks. What is the reduced ratio of spiders to backpacks?

54:9   9:6   6:1   1:6

13. On a 3-night camping trip, 9 campers each slept 4 hours a night. (This is because of all the creatures in their tents!) What is the reduced ratio of total hours of sleep to nights?

a. 3 to 4
b. 36 to 1
c. 4 to 12
d. 27 to 36

14. Dionne found 9 spiders, 5 rats, 3 flies, 18 mosquitoes, and 1 frog in his tent. Which ratio is greater?

a. rats : mosquitoes

b. frog : flies

c. mosquitoes : all critters

d. rats : flies

e. flies : frog

f. spiders : mosquitoes

g. frog : all other critters

15. A trapped squirrel tore up the stuffing in 3 of the 4 sleeping bags in one tent. What is the ratio of damaged to undamaged bags?

a. $\frac{3}{4}$
b. $\frac{4}{1}$
c. $\frac{4}{3}$
d. $\frac{3}{1}$

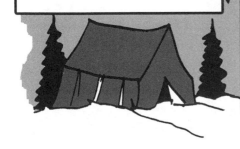

Name _____

Use with page 18.

RATES ON THE TRAIL

A **rate** is a ratio that compares quantities of different units.

When you **reduce** the ratio to an equivalent ratio with the second term of 1, you find the unit rate. This would be the price (or speed, amount, etc.) for each unit. In the example below, peanuts cost $14 per unit (pound) and the speed limit is 10 km per unit (year).

$42/3 lb

10 km/year

Brush up your trail math and find the unit rates.

1. Charlie paid $12.80 for a 4-pound bag of trail mix.

_____ cost per pound

2. Each hiker has the same number of chocolate chips in his or her trail mix bag. There are 120 chips and 8 hikers.

_____ chips per bag

3. A visiting bear ate 144 peanuts in 16 minutes.

_____ peanuts per minute

4. Julianna took 24,240 steps on a 12-km hike.

_____ steps per kilometer

5. 18 hikers drank 126 liters of water.

_____ liters per hiker

6. Carlos took 28 rests in 7 hours of hiking.

_____ rests per hour

7. On a 7-day trek, hikers saw 469 slugs.

_____ slugs per day

Name

RODEO RATES

So far, I think I've cracked about 8 bones per second!

Gallopin' Grady, the great bull rider, is out on the rodeo circuit. You might not expect to find math at a rodeo, but the concept of **rate** is quite important in this setting.

Find unit rates to solve these rodeo problems. Circle the correct answer. Explain to a classmate how you found your answer.

1. Grady has been thrown off the bull 156 times in his last 52 rodeo events. The number of falls per event is:

   a. $\frac{1}{3}$ c. 3
   b. 4   d. 104

2. Grady's recipe for an energy drink has 4 liters of a secret energy ingredient for every 5 liters of spicy tea.

   The amount of secret ingredient in each liter of tea is:

   a. $\frac{1}{4}$ liter   c. $5\frac{1}{4}$ liters
   b. 20 liters   d. 9 liters

3. Rodeo fans pay $150 for season tickets to see 12 rodeos.

   The price of a ticket per rodeo is:

   a. $180   c. $12.00
   b. $8.00   d. $12.50

4. One particularly feisty bucking bull named Hotfoot has thrown 1,800 riders in 120 rodeos.

   The number of riders thrown per rodeo is:

   a. 6   c. 216
   b. 15   d. 20

5. Gallopin' Grady has won 117 events in his last 39 rodeos.

   His number of wins per rodeo is:

   a. 7   c. 4
   b. 0.3   d. 3

6. A bucking bull eats .025 times its body weight per day. Hotfoot eats 45 pounds of food a day.

   Hotfoot's weight is:

   a. 112.5 lb   c. 1,125 lb
   b. 1,800 lb   d. 180 lb

7. A rider must stay on the bull for at least 8 seconds. Hotfoot bucks 17 times during that period of time.

   The number of bucks per second is:

   a. 2.125   c. 5.2
   b. 136   d. 0.47

8. 90 bulls are on hand for today's rodeo. These bulls were valued at a total of $1,530,000.

   The value of each bull is:

   a. $15,300   c. $17,000
   b. $5,000   d. $1,700

Name

Common Core Reinforcement Activities — 6th Grade Math

FLIPS AND WIPEOUTS

Equivalent ratios are ratios that have the same meaning. For example, 1:4 and 2:8 are equivalent ratios because they represent the same relationship. Writing equivalent ratios can help solve many problems. You can show equivalent ratios with the help of a table.

Write equivalent ratios to finish the tables, and they'll lead you right to the skateboarding problem solutions.

1. So far today, Hudson has wiped out 5 times during 12 jumps. At this rate, how many wipeouts would you expect in 72 jumps?

Answer:

Wipeouts	5		20		
Jumps	12				

2. Hudson's sister Maria keeps track of her injuries—even slight ones. So far this year, she's recorded 18 minor injuries in 11 falls. At this rate, how many times would she fall to sustain 108 injuries?

Answer:

Injuries	18		54		
Falls	11				

3. Hudson has practiced a 360-degree flip for months. This week, he did it perfectly 24 out of 54 times. At this rate, how many times out of nine attempts was the flip perfect?

Answer:

Perfect Flips						24
Flip Attempts			27			54

4. Last week, Hudson was on his skateboard 24 hours in comparison to the 16 hours he spent on homework. At this rate, how many hours of skateboarding were done for each hour of homework?

Answer:

Skateboard		3						24
Homework	1	2	4	6	8	10	12	16

Name

Copyright © 2014 World Book, Inc./ Incentive Publications, Chicago, IL

LOBS AND VOLLEYS

Equivalent rates and ratios find their way to the tennis court!

Create one or two tables with equivalent ratios to solve each of these tennis problems.

1. For every 13 of Roxanne's lobs, she hit 7 volleys. At this rate, how many volleys will she hit to get 78 lobs?

Answer:

2. Katrina hit 9 aces out of 54 serves today. Roxanne hit 14 aces out of 70 serves today. Who had the higher ratio of aces to serves?

Answer:

Katrina

Roxanne

3. Jackson spent $25 on food in the $2\frac{1}{2}$ hours he watched the tennis tournament. Liam spent $33 on food in the 3 hours he watched the tournament. Who spent more per half hour?

Answer:

Jackson

Liam

Name

Common Core Reinforcement Activities — 6th Grade Math

BALANCING ACTS

Coordinate planes are great tools for actually "seeing" the solutions to problems. You can use one to solve this balancing problem.

Write equivalent ratios to complete the table and answer the question. Graph the number pairs from the ratios to show the answer.

1. This champion glass-balancer breaks 3 glasses during practice for every 2 balancing tricks he practices. How many glasses would be broken during the practice of 8 tricks?

    Answer:

Broken glasses (x)	0	3				
Tricks (y)	0	2		6		

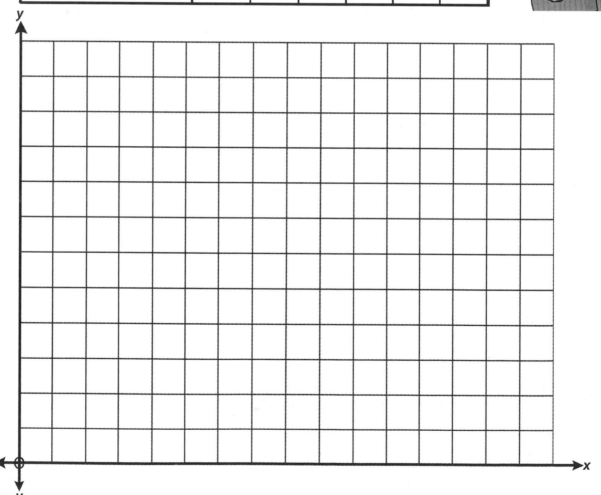

Use with page 25.

Each ratio (2-5) matches one of the lines on the coordinate plane. Write the letter that names the line. (The x-axis represents wobbles. The y-axis represents steps.)

I wobble 8 times for every 4 steps.

_____ 2. 3 wobbles every 5 steps

_____ 3. 8 wobbles every 2 steps

_____ 4. 2 wobbles every 4 steps

_____ 5. 3 wobbles every 2 steps

6. Draw a colored line to show the ratio described in the illustration. Label it E.

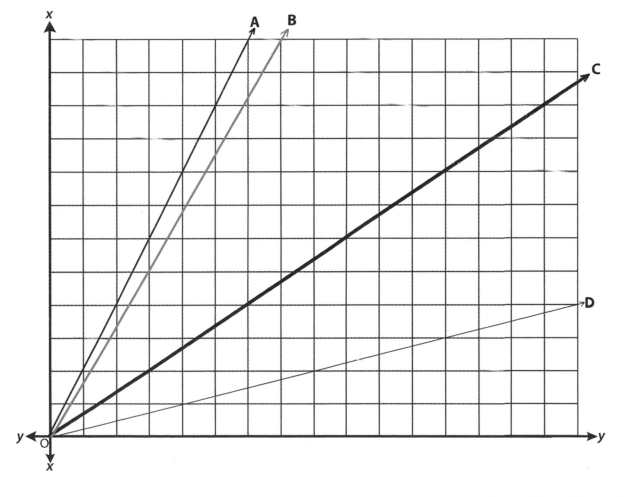

Name

Use with page 24.

Common Core Reinforcement Activities — 6th Grade Math

TRAINS ON THE MOVE

There's hardly a better way to put your understanding of rate to work than solving train problems. Don't get derailed by the tricky questions! Remember that rate multiplied by time equals distance.

Solve the problems to find rates or use rates to find other answers.

1. The *Midnight Express* train takes 9 hours to travel 1,818 kilometers (with no stops).

   a. At that rate, how many kilometers will the train travel in 4 hours? _____

   b. At what rate does the train travel? _____

2. Train A travels 80 miles an hour for 18 hours. Train B travels 85 miles per hour for 16 hours.

   a. Which train travels farther? _____

   b. What is the difference between their distances? _____

3. A train travels 2,100 kilometers at a constant speed, stopping four times for an hour each stop. The total travel time (including the stops) is 18 hours.

   What is the train's speed while moving? _____

4. The dining car on the *West Ghost Cruiser* serves meals seven days a week. The *Cruiser* makes three round trips a day between two small ghost towns. In a week, the chef prepares 6,300 meals.

   How many meals are served on each trip? _____

5. The *ABC Train* travels east at a constant speed. The *XYZ Train* travels west at a constant speed, following a track parallel to the *ABC* track. They each leave their stations, 2,200 miles apart, at exactly the same time. In 14 hours, *ABC* travels 980 miles. In 14 hours, *XYZ* travels 1,050 miles.

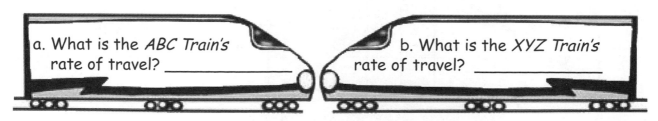

a. What is the *ABC Train's* rate of travel? _____

b. What is the *XYZ Train's* rate of travel? _____

c. Will the trains meet in that 14-hour period?

Solve the problems to find rates or use rates to find other answers.

6. A train travels from Oregon to the Mexican border at a constant rate of speed, covering a distance of 1,230 miles. The train stops 5 times for one hour each time and arrives at its destination in 20 hours total time (including stopping time).

    a. What is the train's speed? _____

    b. If the train continued at the same rate without stopping for 6 more hours, what would be

       the total distance of the trip? _____

7. A train travels at a constant speed, without stopping, for 7 hours and covers a distance of 777 kilometers. A car travels for 9 hours at a constant speed, without stopping, and covers a distance of 945 kilometers.

    a. Which vehicle has the greater speed? _____

    b. If the car continues another hour at the same rate,

       will it cover a total of 1,000 kilometers on its trip? _____

8. A train travels 270 miles up a mountain at a constant speed. The trip takes 6 hours. The same train travels the same route down the mountain at a constant speed. The trip takes 5 hours.

    What is the difference between the rates of speed up and down the mountain? _____

9. A zoo train carried visitors around the zoo grounds, making several trips a day. In 9 trips with all the seats full, it carried 423 passengers.

    a. How many passengers does it take to fill the train? _____

    b. How many full trips would be needed to carry 752 passengers? _____

Name

Use with page 26.

Common Core Reinforcement Activities — 6th Grade Math

JUGGLING PRICES

Chef Henrietta takes time out from her demanding cooking schedule to unwind. Her hobby includes the ability to juggle kitchen items and numbers.

Read the list of ingredients on her shopping list today. Use the information to solve the price problems. Choose a price from the numbers Henrietta is juggling.

SHOPPING LIST

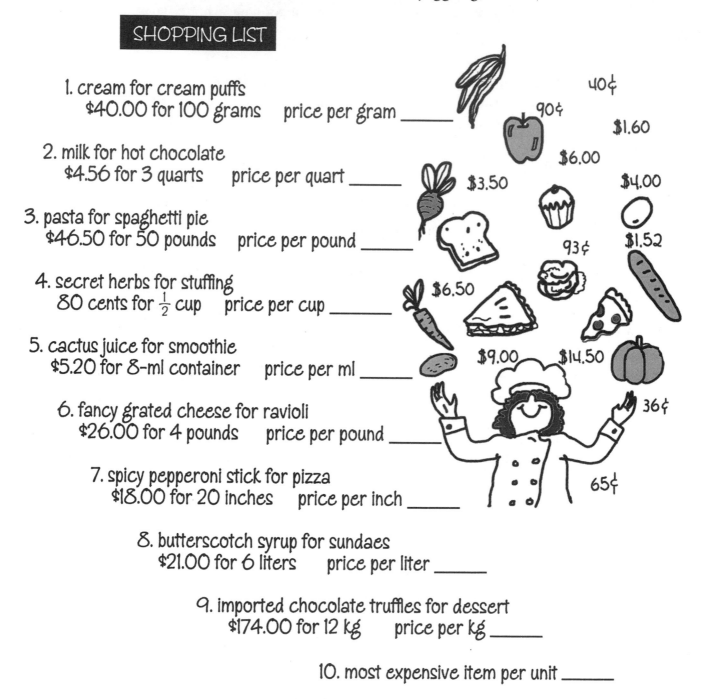

1. cream for cream puffs
   $40.00 for 100 grams   price per gram _____

2. milk for hot chocolate
   $4.56 for 3 quarts   price per quart _____

3. pasta for spaghetti pie
   $46.50 for 50 pounds   price per pound _____

4. secret herbs for stuffing
   80 cents for $\frac{1}{2}$ cup   price per cup _____

5. cactus juice for smoothie
   $5.20 for 8-ml container   price per ml _____

6. fancy grated cheese for ravioli
   $26.00 for 4 pounds   price per pound _____

7. spicy pepperoni stick for pizza
   $18.00 for 20 inches   price per inch _____

8. butterscotch syrup for sundaes
   $21.00 for 6 liters   price per liter _____

9. imported chocolate truffles for dessert
   $174.00 for 12 kg   price per kg _____

10. most expensive item per unit _____

Name

ON TARGET

In many competitions, archers add scores after 6 arrows. Add the scores of these arrows. This total will become a fact needed to calculate some percentages.

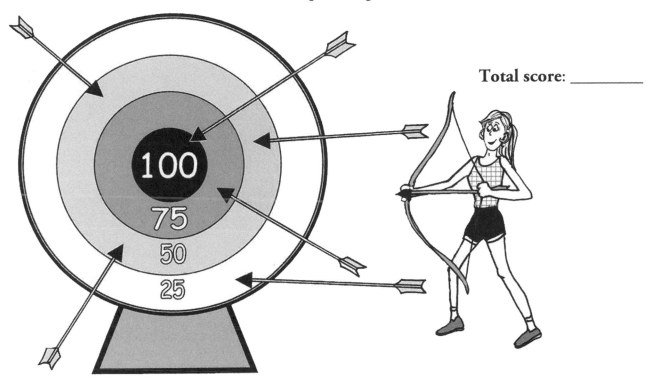

Total score: _____

Find the percentages. Round to the nearest tenth.

1. Percent of arrows scoring 75? _____

2. Percent of arrows scoring 50? _____

3. Percent of arrows scoring 100? _____

4. Percent of the total score from 50s? _____

5. Ring accounting for 21.4% of score? _____

6. Ring accounting for 28.6% of score? _____

7. Ring accounting for about 7.1% of score? _____

Fill in the missing numbers.

8. _____ is 55% of 820.

9. 135 is _____% of 450.

10. 48% of 400 is _____.

11. 594 is _____% of 216.

12. 65% of 200 is _____.

13. 21,000 is 7% of _____.

14. 132 is 165% of _____.

Name

Common Core Reinforcement Activities — 6th Grade Math

IT TAKES A CROWD

Crowds are an important part of sporting events. The fans add to the excitement of any game or competition. It takes a crowd of people to run big sporting events and keep them safe. Sometimes, the game or competition itself involves a crowd of participants!

Solve these problems about sports crowds. Round answers to the nearest tenth.

_____ 1. In 1896, about 300 athletes participated in the first modern Olympic Games in Athens. The 2012 Games in London hosted about 10,500 athletes. Is it accurate to say that the number of 2012 athletes is 3500% of the number of athletes in Athens?

_____ 2. At the 2012 summer Olympics in London, the Olympic Stadium had 80,000 seats. If 78% of the seats were filled 2 hours before the opening ceremony, how many seats were empty at that time?

_____ 3. 10,651 athletes participated in the 2000 Sydney Olympics. Of these, 4,069 were women. What percent of the athletes were men?

_____ 4. In a huge circle dance, 6,748 people joined together to dance the hokey pokey. Assume that 5,061 of these participants had never danced before. What percent would that be?

I'm getting paintball slimed!

_____ 5. A few years ago, 1,356 school children skipped rope at the same time. If 25% of them were over 10 years old, how many would be 10 and under?

_____ 6. Paintball is one of the fastest growing extreme sports in the world with over 12,000,000 players. If 43% of these players are ages 12 to 24, what is the number of players younger than 12 or older than 24?

_____ 7. 962 medals were awarded at the 2012 summer Olympics in London. Australian athletes won 35 medals. What percent is this of the total medals?

Name _____

ARENA STATISTICS

Fans fill arenas for sporting events. Use your skills to solve these percent problems about some fans and activities in arenas.

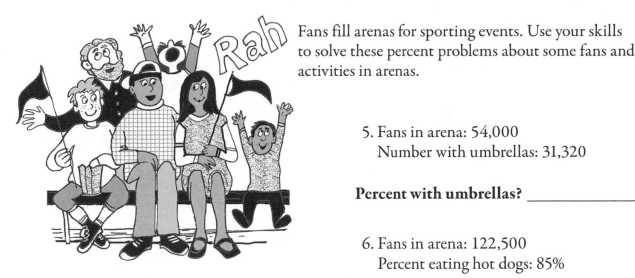

1. The Indianapolis Motor Speedway in Indiana has a greater seating capacity than any other sports arena in the world. Assume a race began with every seat filled, but 65% of the people left during a rainstorm, leaving 140,000 spectators. What is the capacity of the speedway?

Answer: _____

2. A large soccer arena in Mexico City, Mexico, has seating for 104,000. If all seats are full and an additional 25% stand to watch the game, how many spectators will be in the arena?

Answer: _____

3. Fans in arena: 30,800
   Percent wearing team colors: 80%

How many in team colors? _____

4. Fans in arena: 200,000
   Percent standing: 48%

How many sitting? _____

5. Fans in arena: 54,000
   Number with umbrellas: 31,320

Percent with umbrellas? _____

6. Fans in arena: 122,500
   Percent eating hot dogs: 85%

How many eating hot dogs? _____

7. Fans in arena: 4,780
   Number in box seats: 717

Percent in box seats? _____

8. Fans in arena: 97,200
   Number with hoarse voices: 66,096

Percent with hoarse voices? _____

9. 45% of fans cheering for the Hawks.
   Number of fans cheering for the Hawks: 35,325

Total fans in the arena? _____

10. **Fans in the arena:** _____
    Percent waving flags: 60%
    Number waving flags: 50,160

RAH, RAH, RAH!

Name

Common Core Reinforcement Activities — 6th Grade Math

FEED THE TEAM

All that activity has the baseball team members hungry. Five of them have each ordered a hearty meal.

Figure out how much each one will spend. Don't forget the tax and the tip.

MENU

spaghetti......................	$7.90
pizza............................	$12.50
lasagna........................	$13.50
tacos............................	$2.50 ea
enchilada plate............	$6.25
steak and salad............	$16.35
hamburger & fries........	$9.95
milkshake.....................	$4.00
all other drinks.............	$1.50
pie...............................	$3.50

Add 6% tax and 15% tip. Compute both of these based on the subtotal.

FRED

Burger & Fries	___
Steak & Salad	___
Milkshake	___
Subtotal	___
+ Tip	___
+ Tax	___
Total	___

RED

Steak & Salad	___
Enchilada Plate	___
Milkshake	___
Subtotal	___
+ Tip	___
+ Tax	___
Total	___

TAD

2 Burgers & Fries	___
2 Tacos	___
Milkshake	___
Pie	___
Subtotal	___
+ Tip	___
+ Tax	___
Total	___

BRAD

Spaghetti	___
2 Tacos	___
Drink	___
Subtotal	___
+ Tip	___
+ Tax	___
Total	___

CHAD

Lasagna	___
Pizza	___
Milkshake	___
Pie	___
Subtotal	___
+ Tip	___
+ Tax	___
Total	___

Name

WORKOUT CALCULATIONS

At the gym and on the track—measurements are everywhere you look. You'll need a good knowledge of measurement units to solve these workout problems.

Convert the measurement units in each problem.

1. A gym mat was 18 centimeters thick. How many meters? _____

2. Elija ran 6 miles, 1,500 feet on the treadmill. How many feet? ____

3. Alonzo lifted 68 kilograms in weights. How many grams? _____

4. Gavin had 5 pounds, 7 ounces of high-energy snack in his gym bag.
   How many ounces? _____

5. Caitlin drank 1.7 liters of water after her workout.
   How many milliliters? _____

6. A truckload of gym equipment weighed 1.52 metric tons.
   How many kg? _____

7. A truckload of gym equipment weighed 2.5 U.S. tons.
   How many pounds? _____

Circle *yes* or *no* for each question.
If the answer is *no*, write the correct answer.

8. Carlos lifted 50 kilograms. He said it was   yes   no
   5,000 g. Is he right?

9. Lucinda did 120 sit-ups in 263 seconds.   yes   no
   She said it was 2 minutes, 63 seconds.
   Is she right?

10. Jason drank 3 quarts, 2 pints of energy drink.   yes   no
    He said it was 16 cups. Is he right?

11. Kat's bottle holds 1,080 milliliters of   yes   no
    energy drink. She said was 1.8 liters.
    Is she right?

12. Raja sprinted 120 yards, 4 feet.   yes   no
    He said this was 3,640 feet. Is he right?

Use with page 34.

Name

Common Core Reinforcement Activities — 6th Grade Math

WORKOUT CALCULATIONS, continued

Circle the correct answer.

13. Gigi did 85 sit-ups in 2 minutes, 50 seconds. Sam did 32 sit-ups in 48 seconds. Who did sit-ups at a faster rate?

    a. Gigi

    b. Sam

    c. neither (Their rate was the same.)

14. The ABC Gym bought 6 pints of energy powder for $18.90. The BBD Gym bought 3 gallons of the same powder for $72.00. Who got the better deal?

    a. ABC

    b. BBD

    c. neither (They paid the same per pint.)

15. Jamahl skipped rope at a rate of 1,620 skips in 540 seconds. Brad skipped at a rate of 3,360 skips in 28 minutes. Whose rate was faster?

    a. Jamahl

    b. Brad

    c. neither (Their rate was the same.)

16. Team Green drank 8.5 kiloliters of water during the game. Team Blue drank 85 hectoliters during the game. Who drank the most?

    a. Green

    b. Blue

    c. neither (They drank the same amount.)

Calculate or convert the measurements.

17. The water cooler at the gym held 3 gallons of water. (1 gal = 3.791 l) How many liters? _____

18. Bill, Will, and Jill each went for a bike ride, riding the same amount of time each. The total of their times was 8 hours, 45 minutes. How long did each ride? _____

19. Tad's jump rope weighed 12 ounces. (1 oz = 28.35 g) How many grams?_____

20. The perimeter of Joe's mat at the gym was 188 inches. Marilou's mat had a perimeter of 300 centimeters. Whose mat had the greater perimeter? _____

21. Julia's sprint was 138 yards, 2 feet. Jan's sprint was four times as long. How long was Jan's sprint (in yards and feet)?

    _____

22. Aran lifted a 115-pound weight. Greg lifted 88 kilograms. Who lifted more weight?

    _____

Use with page 33.

Name

THE NUMBER SYSTEM

Grade 6

Numerically, this adds up to too many sports!

AMAZING FOOTWORK

All kinds of races get athletes moving on their feet.
Some of these competitions are rather unusual.

**To answer each question, finish the diagram
and solve the equation.**

hop...skip...hop...skip...

3.67

1. Before the three-legged race, Trevor
found $\frac{3}{4}$ of a chocolate bar. He
divided it into pieces that were
$\frac{2}{8}$ of the bar. How many pieces
would he get?

   Solve the problem:

   $\frac{3}{4} \div \frac{2}{8} =$

   **Draw a box around each $\frac{2}{8}$ section
   within the shaded area. (Shaded
   area shows $\frac{3}{4}$ bar.)**

   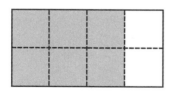

2. The teams of runners have $1\frac{1}{2}$ fields for
practice. Each team needs $\frac{3}{8}$ of a field
for practice space. How many teams can
practice at once?

   Solve the problem:

   $1\frac{1}{2} \div \frac{3}{8} =$

   **Draw a box around each $\frac{3}{8}$ section
   within the shaded area.**

   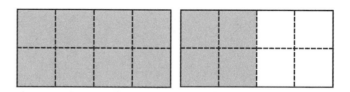

3. Sophie contributes $2\frac{1}{4}$ yards of fabric for leg ties. Each tie must be $\frac{3}{4}$ yard long.
How many ties can be made from her fabric?

   Solve the problem:

   $2\frac{1}{4} \div \frac{3}{4} =$

   Draw a box around each $\frac{3}{4}$ section within the shaded area.

   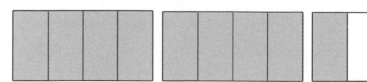

Name

Use with page 37.

Here's another interesting kind of "footwork." People actually enter races pushing things like baby carriages, bathtubs, or vacuum cleaners.

Solve the problems with diagrams and equations.

4. Hans took $1\frac{1}{3}$ energy bars along on his race. He ate portions of $\frac{2}{9}$ bar along the way. How many portions did he have?

    Write an equation that solves the problem.

    Draw and finish a diagram to show the solution.

5. Yesterday Hans had $\frac{4}{5}$ of an hour to train. He ran at three different speeds: fast walk, jog, sprint—each for $\frac{2}{15}$ of an hour. How many segments of training did he fit into the $\frac{4}{5}$ hour?

    Write an equation that solves the problem.

    Draw and finish a diagram to show the solution.

6. At the end of the competition, some friends shared $\frac{6}{7}$ of a cake. Each piece was $\frac{3}{14}$ of that amount of cake. How many people got a piece of cake?

    Write and solve an equation:
    Write an equation that solves the problem.

    Draw and finish a diagram to show the solution.

7. **Write a word problem to match this equation.**

    $\frac{5}{3} \div \frac{1}{16} = 10$

Use with page 36.

Name

DIVISION WORKOUT

Get a workout with your division skills. Tanya keeps a list of tasks for her daily fitness workout. Some of the numbers on her list will be needed for solving the problems.

Write and solve a division problem to find each answer.

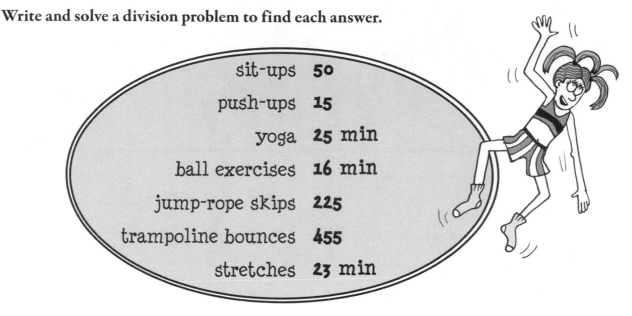

sit-ups	**50**
push-ups	**15**
yoga	**25 min**
ball exercises	**16 min**
jump-rope skips	**225**
trampoline bounces	**455**
stretches	**23 min**

_____ 1. How many workouts will it take Tanya to build up 8,100 minutes of yoga?

_____ 2. How many workouts will it take her to do 15,150 sit-ups?

_____ 3. 336 minutes of ball exercises. How many workouts?

_____ 4. 690 push-ups this month. How many workouts?

_____ 5. 15 hr, 20 min of stretching. How many workouts?

_____ 6. 2,380 rope-skips, resting every 140 skips. How many rests?

_____ 7. Rope skipping at a rate of 720 skips in 6 minutes. Rate per second?

_____ 8. Workout mat: 315 cm long with an area of 170,100 cm^2. The width?

_____ 9. A total of 65,700 trampoline bounces over 18 days. Bounces per day?

_____ 10. Total of 70,280 ml water drunk at a rate of 2,008 ml per workout. How many workouts?

Name _____

DIVIDE AND CONQUER

Karate is a martial art. The word *karate* means *empty hand,* because the athlete practices his or her art without any weapons. Karate is a mixture of punching and kicking techniques. One of the most popular and spectacular moves is the breaking of blocks of wood with the hands, feet, or head.

Use the numbers in the "divided" blocks of wood to sharpen your division skills.

1. 20,608 divided by 64

Quotient_____

2. 3,960 divided by 88

Quotient_____

3. 1,995 divided by 57

Quotient_____

4. 113,220 divided by 204

Quotient_____

5. 502,853 divided by 611

Quotient_____

6. 54,390 divided by 777

Quotient_____

Name_____

FOILED CALCULATIONS

A *foil* is a fencing sword with a flat guard for the hand and a thin blade with a blunt point. The blunt point allows the fighters to practice without getting injured. The word *foil* also means to prevent from being successful.

Two math students, Dominic and Gianna, are taking a short test. Since they are really competitive with one another, each is making a lot of noise, trying to foil the other! The distractions are interfering with their work.

Check both tests. If the answer is wrong, write the correct answer near the problem number. Write *Yes* if the answer is correct.

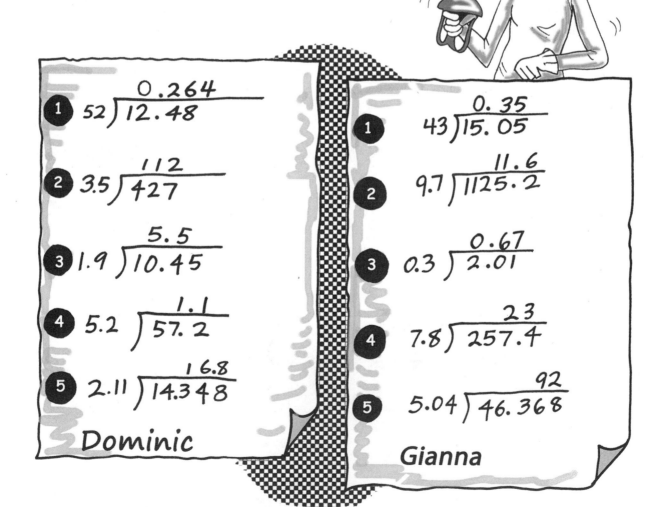

IT TAKES A CREW

The sport of rowing takes strength and discipline. Rowers sit in a *scull* (a light racing boat) and row in singles or crews of two, four, or eight. In 2012, a Canadian team of eight men set a new world record. They completed the 2,000-meter course in 5:19:35 (5 minutes, 19 and 35-hundredths seconds).

Use your skills in operating with decimals to solve these problems. Round answers to nearest thousandths.

1 . In 2012, a German crew set the women's record for quadruple sculls. They covered a 2,000-meter course in 6:09.38. What is the per-second rate of their race?

2. The men's quadruple sculls record was set in 2012 by a team from Russia. They covered the 2,000-meter distance in 5:33.15 minutes. How fast did they travel per second?

3. What was the difference in the women's and men's times (problems 1 and 2)?

Answers

_____

_____

_____

4. A women's crew from China holds the record in quadruple lightweight sculls. The winning time was 6:23.96. What is the difference between this time and the regular quadruple record in problem 1?

5. The total weight of four crewmembers is 301.43 kg. Here are the weights of three of them: 68.15 kg, 75.59 kg, and 77.67 kg. What is the weight of the fourth crewmember?

6. As of early 2014, New Zealander Mahe Drysdale holds the single scull record. His record time is 6:33.35. At the 2012 Summer Olympic Games, he won a gold medal with a time of 6:57.82. How much faster is his world record than the Olympic time?

7. One rower practices by rowing 10,000 meters on Monday. On Tuesday, he rows 0.05 times more distance than Monday. On Wednesday, he rows 0.05 times more distance than on Tuesday. How far does he row on Wednesday?

_____

_____

_____

Name _____

Common Core Reinforcement Activities — 6th Grade Math

MULTIPLES ON THE MOVE

The tallest bicycle (that can be ridden) is about 14 feet tall. If a rider's head and shoulders stand about a foot above the handlebars, this makes the bicycle-rider combination about 15 feet tall. Review and practice multiples and factors. Then find the least common multiple for these two numbers (14 and 15).

Finish the statement between each two wheel spokes.

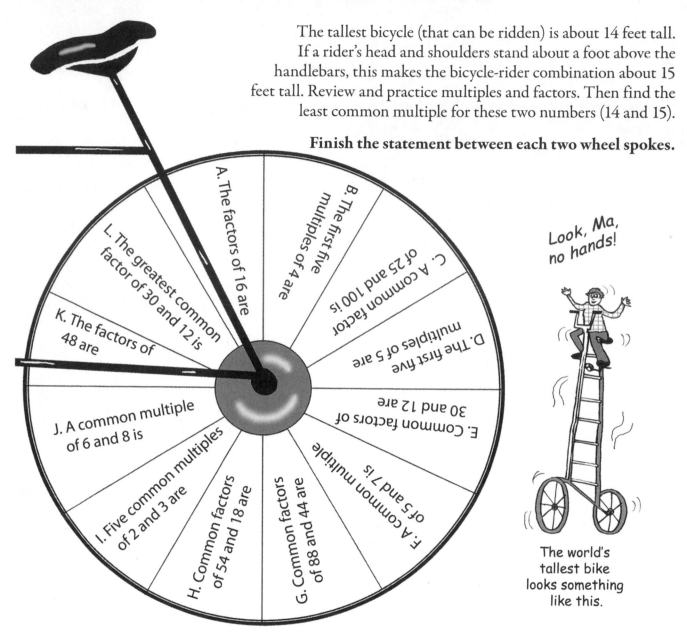

A. The factors of 16 are

B. The first five multiples of 4 are

C. A common factor of 25 and 100 is

D. The first five multiples of 5 are

E. Common factors of 30 and 12 are

F. A common multiple of 5 and 7 is

G. Common factors of 88 and 44 are

H. Common factors of 54 and 18 are

I. Five common multiples of 2 and 3 are

J. A common multiple of 6 and 8 is

K. The factors of 48 are

L. The greatest common factor of 30 and 12 is

Look, Ma, no hands!

The world's tallest bike looks something like this.

M. The greatest common factor of 40 and 72 is

N. The least common multiple of 4 and 5 is

O. The least common multiple of 4 and 6 is

P. The least common multiple of 12 and 9 is

Q. The greatest common factor of 32 and 80 is

R. Show how you found the least common multiple of 14 and 15.

S. A common multiple of 2 and 9 is

Name

SOMETHING IN COMMON

Factors and multiples meet real life. To solve these everyday problems, you'll need to be skilled at finding greatest common factors and least common multiples.

Solve the problems. Then label each one LCM (least common multiple) or GCF (greatest common factor) on the line before the problem. This will show which of these you had to find to solve the problem. Draw sketches or diagrams if you need them to help find your solutions.

_____ 1. Tatiana arranges sets of towels and water bottles to place around the locker room. She has 36 towels and 28 bottles. How many identical sets can she create, and what is in each set?

_____ 2. There's a strange smell coming from a locker. The lockers are numbered 1 through 50. Coach Sal checks every sixth locker. Coach Val checks every eighth locker. Which is the first locker both will check?

_____ 3. The sixth graders have a math test and a science test today. They have a science test every 9 school days and a math test every 6 school days. In how many days will tests fall on the same day again?

_____ 4. On the weekend, the team gathers for pizza. The pizza comes sliced in 12 slices. The drinks come packaged in sets of 8 cans. How many pizzas and sets of drinks will they need to buy to get the same number of pizza slices and drinks?

_____ 5. Tatiana wants to give a box of chocolates to each of her friends. She has 42 milk chocolates and 12 white chocolates. What is the greatest number of identical boxes she can create using all the chocolates? How many of each type will be in each box?

_____ 6. Lucas has two licorice ropes—21 feet long and 3 feet long. He wants to cut as many pieces the same length as he can with no waste. What is the greatest length he should cut the pieces so that each friend gets the same size licorice rope?

_____ How many pieces will he get?

_____ 7. To get ready for the picnic on Saturday, Annie buys hot dogs and rolls. Rolls come in packages of 8. Hot dogs come in packages of 10. What is the least number of packages of each that can be bought to make hot dogs in rolls without having any of either left over?

Name _____

Common Core Reinforcement Activities — 6th Grade Math

HEAVY LIFTING

Take away some of the heavy lifting of addition by factoring out common factors from the addends. Give it a try!

> Example: $85 + 15 = 5(17 + 3)$
>
> Factor out 5—the greatest common factor of 85 and 15. Use the distributive property to express the sum as a multiple of two numbers with no common factor.

Use the distributive property to express each sum as a multiple of a sum of two numbers with no common factor other than 1. (One of the factors on the weights should help with each problem!) Then solve the problem.

	Rewrite the problem.	Sum
1	99 + 54 =	
2	45 + 90 =	
3	63 + 84 =	
4	144 + 36 =	
5	77 + 22 =	
6	96 + 21 =	
7	16 + 56 =	
8	90 + 48 =	
9	24 + 72 =	
10	21 + 84 =	

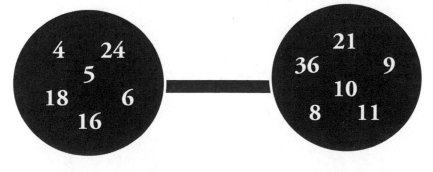

Name

FROSTY NUMBERS

The temperatures are chilling out on the frozen lake. Use your understanding of positive and negative numbers to solve these frosty problems.

Write an answer to each question.

1. What number represents the temperature twelve degrees below zero Celsius?

2. What number represents the temperature two degrees above zero Celsius?

3. Which temperature is warmer: -27 °C or -18 °C?

4. What temperature is 20 ° colder than 6 °Celsius?

5. On Monday, the temperature was 4 °C. On Tuesday, the temperature was -31 °C. Charlie said the temperature had fallen 27°. Was he right?

6. What is the meaning of zero in 1-5 above?

7. A duck flew over Charlie's head at a height of 15 meters above the ice. With zero representing the top of the ice surface on the lake, what number represents the duck's location?

8. A fish swam near Charlie's hook 4 meters below the surface. With zero representing the top of the ice surface on the lake, what number represents the fish's depth?

9. If the duck is directly above the fish in problems 6 and 7, what is the distance between them?
   a. 11 meters   c. -11 meters
   b. 19 meters   d. -19 meters

10. Another fish swims 20 feet below the top ice surface. What number represents its location?

Name _____

Common Core Reinforcement Activities — 6th Grade Math

NUMBERS TAKE A DIVE

Positive and negative numbers come in handy during those diving descents and ascents.

Write a number on the bubble to represent the location or amount.

1. The deck of the diver's boat is fourteen feet above sea level.

2. When the diver descends thirty-six and five-tenths feet below the surface.

1

2

3

3. An octopus lurks at forty feet below the surface.

4. A seagull soars eighty-seven feet above the boat deck.

4

5

5. A lobster crawls on the ocean floor, sixty-five feet below the surface.

6. Marcy dives to -28 feet. Marcus dives ten feet deeper.

6

7

7. The water temperature is sixty-seven degrees Fahrenheit.

8

8. To pay for her scuba equipment, Marcy overdrew her bank account by seventy-five dollars.

9

9. A diver is forty-six feet in vertical distance below the sea level.

10. Liam climbs the vertical sailboat mast. It is twenty-three feet above sea level.

11

10

11. A diver descends 95 feet below the surface. Then she heads straight upwards a distance of 15 feet. She spies a shipwreck and descends 30 feet. What is her location now in relation to the surface?

Name _____

WHO'S WHERE?

Positive and negative numbers can help identify where someone is in relation to a set place (labeled zero) or to others.

Zero represents the place on the rock wall where the climbers began their climb today. Use the vertical number line to answer 1-4.

1. What climber's position has a value opposite from the value of Ty's position?

2. What other climbers are at locations that represent opposites?

3. What is Devon's location?

4. If the numbers represent meters, what is the distance between Suki's and Lucy's positions?

Zero represents the race's starting point. Michael started behind due to a pre-race penalty. Use the horizontal number line to answer 5-10.

5. What is Michael's location?

6. What is Jana's location?

7. Describe the relationship between their locations.

8. What is the opposite of -4?

9. What is the opposite of the opposite of -4?

10. Draw a biker at -3.5.

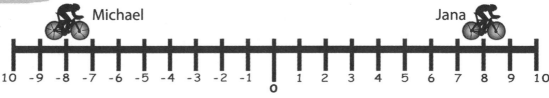

Name

Common Core Reinforcement Activities — 6th Grade Math

ANT INVASIONS

A picnic blanket was set out after a soccer game, but the ants invaded and delayed the picnic. **An ordered pair of numbers can indicate the location of each ant.**

Figure out which ant is where! Fill in the missing information below the grid.

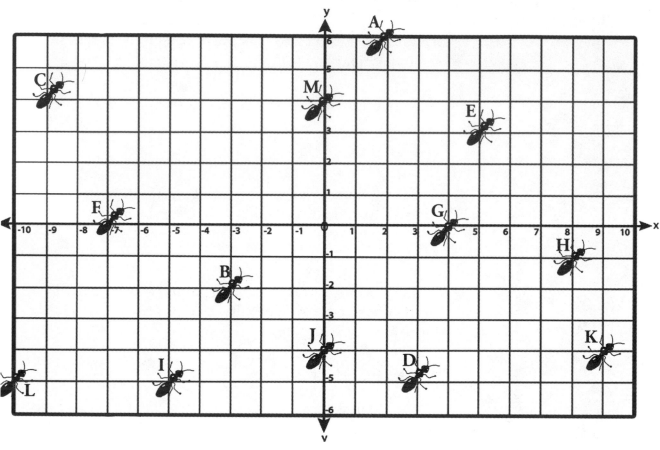

1. Location of ant A?

2. Ant at (3, -5)?

3. (6, -6) would be in which quadrant?

4. Ant at (-3, -2)?

5. Location of ant K?

6. Draw an ant at (-5, 3). Label it P.

7. Location of ant F?

8. Location of ant H?

9. Ant at (0, 4)?

10. (-2, -6) would be in which quadrant?

11. Ant at (5, 3)?

12. Location of ant D?

13. Draw an ant at (0, -6). Label it Q.

14. Ant at (-9, 4)?

Name _____

Use with page 49.

48

Use the coordinate planes to locate and position ordered pairs and figures.

GRID A

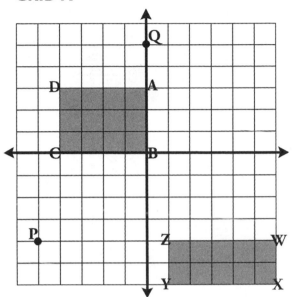

1. Napkin ABCD, placed on the table cloth (coordinate plane) blew to a new location. This location is its original location reflected across the y-axis. Draw ABCD in its new location. Label the corners A_1, B_1, C_1, D_1.

2. Napkin WXYZ blew to a location that is a reflection from its original location across the x-axis. Draw WXYZ in its new location. Label the corners W_1, X_1, Y_1, Z_1.

3. Reflect point P across both axes. Its new locations are

4. Reflect point Q across the x-axis. Its new location is

GRID B

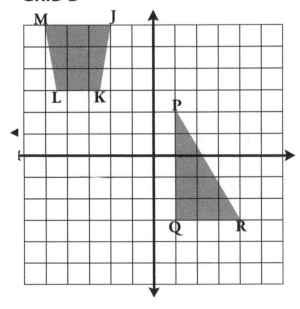

5. Napkin JKLM blew to a location that is a reflection of its original location across the y-axis. Draw JKLM in its new location. Label the corners J_1, K_1, L_1, M_1.

6. Napkin PQR blew to a location that is a reflection of its original location across the y-axis. Draw PQR in its new location. Label the corners P_1, Q_1, R_1.

7. A figure has these points.
   S (-1, -1); T (-8, -1); U (-8, -5)
   When the figure is reflected across the x-axis, what will be the new location for point U?

Name

Use with page 48.

Common Core Reinforcement Activities — 6th Grade Math

FALLING FROM THE SKY

Parachutes are everywhere. Line graphs can help locate the falling skydivers during their fall and after their landings.

Use the vertical graph to answer questions 1-5.

1. What is the opposite of the location of skydiver A?

2. Which skydiver is located at the opposite of -1?

3. What is the location of skydiver C?

4. What is the opposite of skydiver D's location?

5. Draw a parachute at the opposite location of E. Label it M.

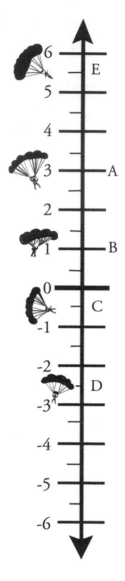

Use the horizontal graph to answer questions 6-10.

6. What is the opposite of the location of skydiver X?

7. Which skydiver landed at -2.2?

8. Which skydiver landed at $1\frac{4}{5}$?

9. Where did skydiver Y land?

10. Draw a parachute to show that skydiver Z landed at -1.6.

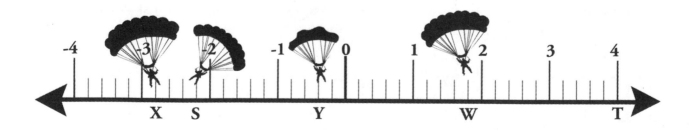

Name

SHOCK ON THE SLOPES

A skier was so shocked by what she saw on the slopes that she lost control!

Position the number pairs on the grid. Then connect them in order to see what surprised the skier.

A	(1, 9)	O	(-0.5, -9)
B	(2, 8.5)	P	(-3.5, -9)
C	(2.5, 7)	Q	(-3, -6)
D	(2, 6)	R	(-4, -4)
E	(6, 3)	S	(-4, 0)
F	(6, 2)	T	(-3, 3)
G	(4, 2)	U	(-4, 2)
H	(3, 3)	V	(-6, 2)
I	(4, 0)	W	(-6, 3)
J	(4, -4)	X	(-2, 6)
K	(3, -6)	Y	(-2.5, 7)
L	(3.5, -9)	Z	(-2, 8.5)
M	(0.5, -9)	XX	(-1, 9)
N	(0, -6)	YY	(same as A)

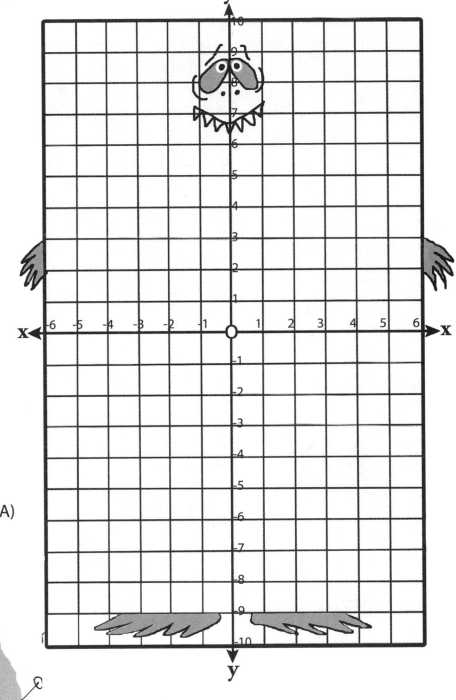

Common Core Reinforcement Activities — 6th Grade Math

THE CHASE IS ON!

The number line helps to tell the story of a swimmer racing for a boat and a curious shark racing for the swimmer.

Match the numerical statements below the number line to the written statements above the number line. (Write the correct statement on the line.)

_____ 1. The boat at 350 ft is to the right of the swimmer at zero on the number line.

_____ 2. The swimmer at zero is behind the boat at 350.

_____ 3. The shark at -500 is to the left of the swimmer at 0 on the number line.

_____ 4. The boat at 350 ft is to the right of the shark at -500 on the number line.

_____ 5. The shark at -500 is to the left of the boat at 350 on the number line.

_____ 6. The swimmer at zero is to the right of the shark at -500 on the number line.

$-500 < 0$ $500 < 350$

$350 > 0$ $-500 < 350$

$350 > -500$

$350 < 500$ $0 < 350$ $0 > -500$

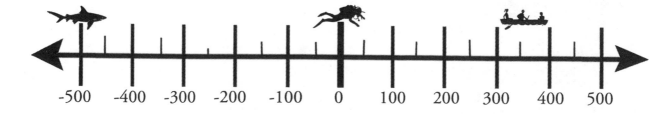

Name

A NEED FOR NUMBERS

Whether athletes are at the gym, on a track, in the street, or on the water—they can't escape math. Numbers help to explain what's going on during almost any sporting venture.

Write statements of order for numbers in these situations. Use > or < symbols to compare and order the numbers.

1. A surfer takes a dive 2 feet below the surface of the water while a parasailor soars 22 feet above the water's surface.

   Numerical statement: _____

2. Six months ago at Tom's snowboard competition, the temperature was -14 °C. Today, during the skateboard event, the temperature was 22 °C.

   Numerical statement: _____

3. When the snowboard competition began, the temperature was -14 °C, but by the time it ended, the temperature had warmed up to -6 °C!

   Numerical statement: _____

4. Brooklyn has saved $80 for new skating equipment. Lola owes the bank $60 for her last pair of new skates.

   Numerical statement: _____

Explain these statements of order for numbers.

5. -$35 < $48 _____

6. 0 > -55 > -59 _____

7. 5 °C > -15 °C _____

8. -18 < -8 _____

9. 6.8 > -20.5 _____

Name _____

ORDER ON THE RINGS

In the 2012 Summer Olympics, Cyril Tommasone of France scored 14.400 points on the rings in the Men's Individual All-Around gymnastics competition. Danell Leyva, of the USA, scored 14.733 on the rings in the same event. Kohei Uchimura of Japan scored 15.333 on the rings in the same event. This inequality describes the relationship of these scores:

$$14.400 < 14.733 < 15.333$$

Circle or write an answer for each problem.

1.
Is the statement true about these scores?

$15.803 < 15.81 < 15.811$

2.
Write these amounts in order from least to greatest:

$150

-$155 $150.55

3.
After traveling to competitions, Lu has -$400 in his bank account. Lee has $35, and Len has -$275. Which statement reflects this situation?

a. -$400 < $35 < $275
b. $35 > -$400 > $-275
c. -$400 < $-275 < $35

4.
Write these numbers in order from least to greatest:

$-\frac{7}{9}$ 0.9 $-3\frac{1}{4}$

5.
Which is true?

a. $36.8 < 36\frac{4}{5}$

b. $36.8 > 36\frac{4}{5}$

c. $36.8 = 36\frac{4}{5}$

6.
Write these numbers in order from least to greatest:

$\frac{1}{5}$ $\frac{-20}{30}$ -0.5

7.
Which is true?

a. $5\frac{1}{2} > 5\frac{3}{8}$
b. $5\frac{1}{2} < 5\frac{3}{8}$
c. $5\frac{1}{2} = 5\frac{3}{8}$

8.
Write these temperatures in order from least to greatest:

0.85 $8\frac{3}{4}$ -8.05

Name

A GAME OF ABSOLUTES

Many times, a football play ends behind the spot on the field where the play began. This could be expressed with a negative number (-12.5 yards). But when we talk about it, we use the absolute value of the number and say there was a loss of 12.5 yards on the play.

Write a phrase (in words) to express these negative values.

1. $-22\frac{1}{2}$ yards on the play

_____

2. team's bank account balance: -$250

_____

3. temperature of -5 °F at time of game

_____

4. team bus drove -20 km/hr in relation to the speed limit

_____

Find the value of each expression.

5. $\left|-\frac{3}{4}\right|$

6. $|\$89.75|$

7. $|-0.76|$

8. $\left|\frac{20}{27}\right|$

9. $|-65.4|$

10. $|-37|$

Solve the problems.

11. $|-8| - |8| =$

12. $|-15| + |20| =$

13. $20.5 + |-15| =$

14. Is this true: $|-5| < 5$?

15. Is this true: $0 + |-8| = 8$?

16. How many numbers are 8.8 units from zero on a number line?

Name

Common Core Reinforcement Activities — 6th Grade Math

SCUBA FINANCES

Scuba diver Lucas has made many purchases to outfit himself for his favorite sport. Use your understanding of absolute value to answer these questions about his scuba debt.

Finish the statements.

1. Last month, he charged the regulator and tanks.

   $|-300| + |-600|$

   Debt for this purchase is

2. Last week, he charged the wet suit, fins, and boots.

   $|-800| + |-100| + |-50|$

   Debt for this purchase is

3. Yesterday, his bank account balance was $98. He wrote a check for his purchase of the knife and gloves.

a. Bank account balance after these purchases is

b. Debt owed the bank after these purchases is

Write T (true) or F (false) for each of these statements.

_____ 4. -50 < 0

_____ 5. |-50| < 0

_____ 6. Lucas bought the snorkel and mask. He had a gift card from the scuba store for $35. This statement represents the amount he owes:

   $(|-50| + |-200|) - 35 = |215|$

_____ 7. When Lucas tried out his new gear, he jumped from the boat deck 8 feet above sea level and dove to -27 feet. This statement represents the distance of his jump and dive in feet.

   $|8| + |-27| = |19|$

HOOD $50.
SNORKEL $50.
REGULATOR $300.
MASK $200.
TANKS $600.
GLOVES $50.
GAUGES $400.
KNIFE $100.
WET SUIT $800.
BOOTS $50.
FINS $100.

Name

TREASURE ON THE GRID

The coordinate plane (grid) pictured here includes a map fit for a treasure hunt. A treasure hunter lands at point A on the island. She hikes to each of the locations shown by coordinates below and digs for treasure at each spot.

Draw her trail from point to point, beginning at point A and moving in the alphabetical order given below. Draw an X at each place she digs. She finds the treasure at the last location. Draw a treasure chest there.

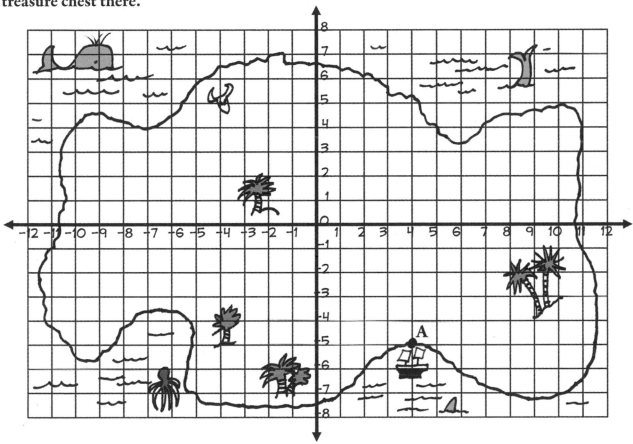

She digs for treasure at these sites, moving alphabetically:

B (4, -3)	C (0, -4)	D (-4, -5)
E (0, -2)	F (2, 4)	G (-9, 2)
H (-9, -3)	I (0, 0)	J (8, 0)
K (10, 2)	L (10, -6)	M (7, -3)

1. If each square represents a square kilometer, is the treasure more than 5 kilometers from point A?

2. What animal can be found at (-9, 7)?

Name

Common Core Reinforcement Activities — 6th Grade Math

SPORTS STUFF GALORE

Speed skater Lara is a sports fanatic. She gets involved in every sport she possibly can. You can imagine how much sporting equipment she has collected! The coordinate plane represents the floor of her room. You can use it to find and graph points that locate some of her belongings.

Use this coordinate plane to answer the questions and follow the directions on the next page, page 59.

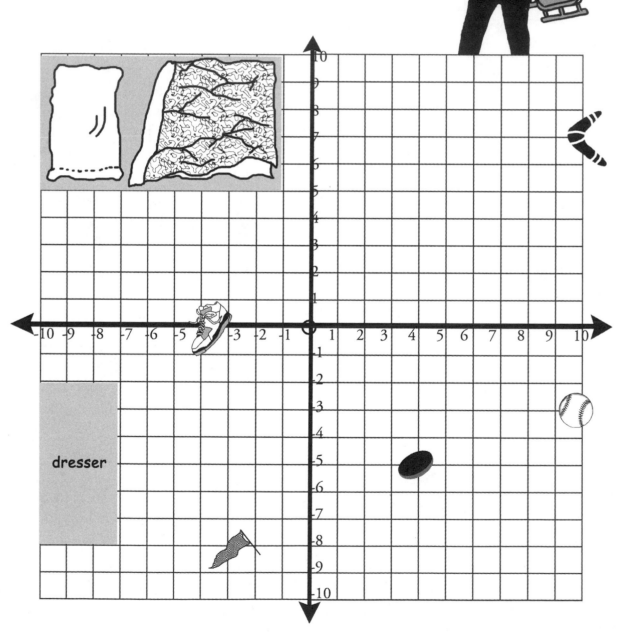

Name

Use with page 59.

Real-World Problems, Coordinate Plane

Use the coordinate plane on page 58 to answer the questions and follow the directions. Write number pairs to give locations of points on the grid.

1. Which of these points falls beneath the bed?

   a. (3, 6)

   b. (-3, 6)

   c. (3, -6)

2. Where is the black hockey puck?

3. Where is the running shoe?

4. What is at (10, -3)?

5. Draw a stopwatch at (0, -7).

6. Draw a football at (6, 5).

7. Draw a flag at (5, 0).

8. Draw a skate at (-10, -4).

9. Draw a boxing glove at (-8, 2).

10. Draw a soccer ball at the origin.

11. Draw a helmet (-9, -6).

12. Draw golf balls at (7, -6) and (-6, -7).

13. If each square represents a square foot, what is the straight distance from the puck to the edge of the dresser?

14. What is the distance from the boomerang to the baseball?

15. What is the distance from the tennis ball to the stopwatch?

16. What is the distance from the football to a point at (6, -9)?

17. Is this statement true? The distance between the golf balls is greater than 12 feet.

18. Draw a 12-unit straight line from the hockey puck into Quadrant I.

Name

Use with page 58.

Common Core Reinforcement Activities — 6th Grade Math

WHERE DID THAT LAND?

It was a great hit. Now where did it land?

Answer these questions about stray softballs. Use the coordinate plane for reference.

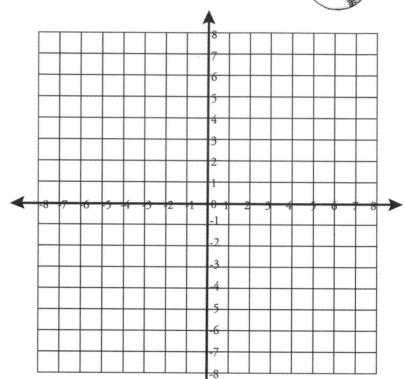

1. One ball landed at (-8, 4). In what quadrant did it fall?

2. Another ball landed at (7, -6.5). In what quadrant did it fall?

3. Two balls landed at these locations: A (-5, -5) and B (5, 5). Which is in Quadrant III?

4. A ball landed 10 units away (on a straight horizontal path in Quadrant I) from (-3, 6). Where did it land?

5. Another ball traveled 12 units on a straight vertical line from (3, 5) across the x-axis. Where did it land?

6. Three balls fell near each other. Their locations were: R (0, 6); S (-8, 0); and T (0, 0). They each rolled two units to the right. Where are they now?

7. What is the distance between a ball at (-8, 7) and one at (-8, -6)?

8. What is the distance between a ball at (7, -7) and one at (-5, -7)?

9. What is the distance between a ball at (6, 0) and one at (-3, 0)?

10. A cardboard box fell on the field with its four corners at these locations:
W (9, -2)   X (1, -2)
Y (1, -8)   Z (9, -8)
What is the perimeter of the surface of the box that touches the field?

Name _____

EXPRESSIONS AND EQUATIONS

Grade 6

My arm strength is
not equal to
the weight of
this wood.

WHO'S RELATED?

Some of the hikers are related to each other. Find out about some of these relationships while you explore relationships between the numbers that describe their sizes and weights. The weights of each hiker include the weight of the person and the full pack.

MATT
Age: 8
Weight: 80 lb
Boot Size: 2

CHAD
Age: 15
Weight: 180 lb
Boot Size: 12

MIKE
Age: 18
Weight: 200 lb
Boot Size: 10

BASHA
Age: 16
Weight: 130 lb
Boot Size: 7

TONI
Age: 12
Weight: 120 lb
Boot Size: 6

Solve the problem to find who is related to whom.

1. The square of Basha's age is 192 greater than the square of her cousin's age. Who is Basha's cousin?

2. The square of Mike's weight is 33,600 greater than the square of his brother's weight. Who is Mike's brother?

3. When Chad's sister's boot size is raised to the fourth power, the result is 432 less than Chad's boot size raised to the third power. Who is Chad's sister?

Write the expressions with exponents.

4. 6 multiplied by itself 9 times

5. the square of the sum of 3 and 15

6. Write 625 as an exponent with a base of 5.

7. Write -243 with a base of -3.

8. In 2013, the population of France was around 64^6 people. Write this population without using an exponent.

Evaluate these expressions.

9. $\left(\frac{2}{4}\right)^4 =$

10. $(0.25)^3 =$

11. $-100^5 =$

12. $\left(\frac{3}{5}\right)^1 =$

13. $\left(\frac{1}{3}\right)^3 + 3^3 =$

14. $\left(\frac{4}{7}\right)^0 =$

Name

A SIMPLE TASK?

Setting up a tent ought to be simple for an experienced camper, right? That's not quite the story for Chad, who's having severe tent trouble today. It took him a long time to get it right (5^3 minutes, to be exact)! It took Basha 3^3 minutes. Toni set up her tent in 4^2 minutes. Zoey took 2^3 minutes. Matt beat them all by setting up his tent in 121 minutes less than Chad. This expression shows how much time was spent setting up tents today.

$$5^3 + 3^3 + 4^2 + 2^3 + (5^3 - 121) =$$

Oh! I just give up!

Chad

1. Evaluate the expression above to find out how much time each camper spent setting up his or her tent.

Chad _____   Zoey _____

Basha _____   Matt _____

Toni _____   Total time _____

Explain the expressions.

2. $4y - 2y^2$

3. x^8

4. $(-6 + 3)^3$

Write an expression to match the words.

5. 10 to the sixth power divided by 5

6. negative one-half to the third power

7. the square of the sum of 18 and 3

Evaluate each expression. Circle the right answer.

8. $(2^3)(5^2)$ 100,000   200   16,807

9. $(3n)^3 + 2^3$ $27n^3 + 8$ $125n^3$ $9n + 6$

10. $(-\frac{2}{5})^3$ $-\frac{6}{5}$ $-\frac{8}{15}$ $-\frac{8}{125}$

11. 72^0 -72   0   1

12. $(4 + 6)^6$ 1,000,000   6,000,000 46^6

13. $100 - 8^2$ 8,464   10,064   36

14. -2^5 -32   32   -10

15. -6^3 -18   -216   216

16. $a^6 + 8a^6 - 2a^6$ 279,936 $7a^6$ 7

Name _____

Common Core Reinforcement Activities — 6th Grade Math

EXPRESSIONS TO BOOT

At the end of a long day of hiking, hikers quickly pull boots off hot, aching feet. Use the boot statistics to practice your skills reading and writing expressions.

Sam's boots are 3 sizes less than twice the size of Toni's.
One of these equations represents his boot size.
Which one is it? (Circle it.)
(s = Sam's boot size; t = Toni's size)

$$s = t - 3$$
$$s = 2(3-t)$$
$$s = 2t - 3$$
$$t = 2s + 3$$

Circle the correct expression for each statement.

1. Basha's boots (b) cost $80 more than Chad's. The cost of Chad's boots was

   a. $b < 80$ b. $b + 80$ c. $b - 80$

2. Toni's boots cost $5 less than twice the cost of Sam's (s). The cost of Toni's boots was

   a. $2s - 5$ b. $s + (2)(5)$ c. $5 - 2s$

3. Zoey's new boots cost $8 more than Toni's (t) and Chad's (c) combined. The cost of Zoey's boots was

   a. $8 - (t + c)$ b. $t + c > 8$ c. $(t + c) + 8$

4. Toni dried out her boots 4 hours longer on Friday than on Thursday (t). The time she dried her boots on Friday was

   a. $t - 4$ b. $t + 4$ c. $4t$

5. There are twice as many holes in Chad's socks (c) as there are in Toni's socks. The number of holes in Toni's socks is

   a. $\frac{c}{2}$ b. $2c$ c. $c + 2$

6. On Sunday (s), Chad's boots (and Chad wearing them!) traveled several kilometers. On Monday (m), they traveled two kilometers fewer in distance than the square of Sunday's distance. The distance they traveled on Monday is

   a. $m < s + 2$ b. $s^2 - 2$ c. $s^2 + m + 2$

7. Sam has 8 more than 4 times as many blisters on his left foot (l) as on his right (r). The number of blisters on his left foot is

   a. $8r + 4$ b. $4r + 8$ c. $8r - 4$

8. The table shows how the number of blisters on Mike's right foot (r) changed as the number of blisters on his left foot (l) changed. Which expression shows the situation?

   a. $l + r > 10$

   b. $r + 2 = 1$

   c. $2l + 1 = r$

left (l)	right (r)
1	3
2	5
3	7
4	9
5	11
6	13
7	15
8	17

Name

EXPRESSIONS WITH TASTE

No hiker wants to carry a back-breaking pack, so most pay attention to the weight of the supplies gathered for a trip. The weights in ounces of each food item are represented by letter symbols on the chart.

For example:
the weight of five boxes of raisins increased by the weight of eight chocolate bars is written

$$5r + 8c$$

These chocolate bars weigh a lot. I'd better get rid of them all!

CAMPING FOOD

weight in ounces	food
m	maple oatmeal
n	noodle packs
s	cans of stew
a	apples
h	hot chocolate packs
r	boxes of raisins
c	chocolate bars
t	bags of trail mix
f	fruit leather sticks
b	bread rolls
j	jerky sticks
p	power bars

Use the letter symbols to write algebraic expressions to match these word expressions.

Write an expression to show the weight of:

1. 1 bag of maple oatmeal increased by 3 ounces

2. 15 boxes of raisins decreased by 7 jerky sticks

3. 4 power bars decreased by 2 packs of noodles

4. 12 bags of trail mix decreased by 4 bags of trail mix

5. 8 chocolate bars decreased by 5 ounces

6. twice the sum of 2 bread rolls and 6 jerky sticks

7. 3 times the difference between 2 stew cans and 5 fruit leather sticks

8. 10 hot chocolate packets increased by 1 stew can and 2 power bars

9. 2 apples weigh less than 3 power bars

10. 5 times the weight of a bread roll and an apple

11. the sum of $\frac{1}{2}$ bag of raisins and $\frac{1}{4}$ bag of trail mix

12. 10 times the combined weight of one bread roll and one fruit leather weighs more than 5 apples

Name

ALGEBRA ON THE TRAIL

Study the route the hikers plan to take to the summit of Mt. Blister. On the first day, they plan to hike from the trailhead to Lake Achoo. The second day, they'll go on to Horsefly Pond. On Day Three, their trip will take them past the Fire Lookout and Moose Lake to a campground at Bear Cave. On the last day, they'll climb to the Mt. Blister summit.

This expression represents their trip for the first two days:

x + y + 2.5y + 2x + 3

There are two different variables: x and y.
There are five terms: x, y, 2.5y, 2x, and 3.
x and 2x are like terms. y and 2.5y are like terms.
x and y and 3 are unlike terms.
3 is the coefficient of 3x.

How many variables in each expression?

_____ 1. $2z - 9x$

_____ 2. $-4b + 2a + -7a^2$

_____ 3. $-9k + 2m$

_____ 4. $p + q + 2(r - s)$

Are the terms like (L) or unlike (U)?

_____ 5. $6x + 17x - 2x$

_____ 6. $14y + 6x - x$

_____ 7. $-3a + 2(c + b)$

_____ 8. $-20 p + 6q$

How many terms in each expression?

_____ 9. $y + \frac{1}{2} y$

_____ 10. $-10p + 2\frac{1}{2} q + r - s$

_____ 11. $2x + 3y + 9.9z + w$

_____ 12. $3.5p$

$$7z + \frac{18m}{2} + \frac{1}{2} b + z$$

13. What are the terms in this expression?

_____

14. Which are like terms? _____

15. What is the coefficient of **m**? _____

16. What is the coefficient of **b**? _____

Name _____

CLIMBING SOLUTIONS

Scale the rock wall along with these climbers by reading and examining the expressions.

Write the letters of expressions that contain the features named in the right-hand column.

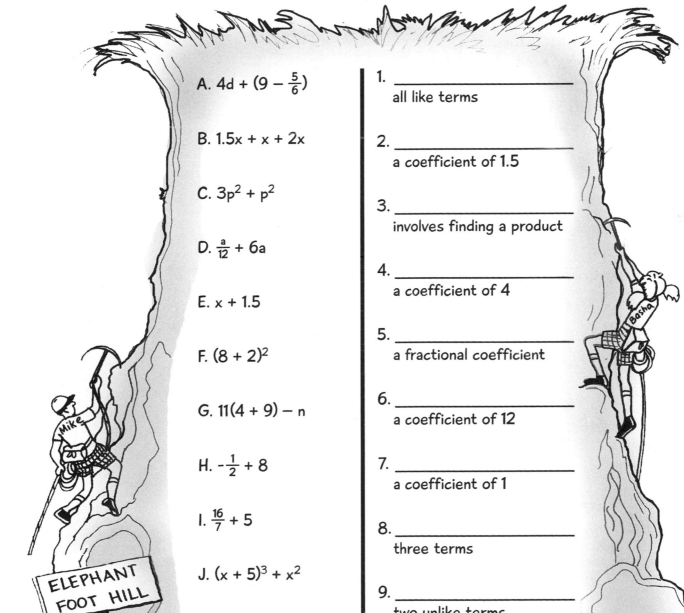

A. $4d + (9 - \frac{5}{6})$

B. $1.5x + x + 2x$

C. $3p^2 + p^2$

D. $\frac{a}{12} + 6a$

E. $x + 1.5$

F. $(8 + 2)^2$

G. $11(4 + 9) - n$

H. $-\frac{1}{2} + 8$

I. $\frac{16}{7} + 5$

J. $(x + 5)^3 + x^2$

K. $c(13 - 7)$

L. $12b - 4.5b$

1. _____
   all like terms

2. _____
   a coefficient of 1.5

3. _____
   involves finding a product

4. _____
   a coefficient of 4

5. _____
   a fractional coefficient

6. _____
   a coefficient of 12

7. _____
   a coefficient of 1

8. _____
   three terms

9. _____
   two unlike terms

10. _____
    one or more exponential terms

Name

Common Core Reinforcement Activities — 6th Grade Math

TRUE EXPRESSIONS

4w < c + b !

This sentence makes sense to the shoppers. With a look at the list of camping goods, it will make sense to you, too. (Notice the money value of each letter variable.) It's an expression that uses numbers instead of words to tell you something. In this case, it tells you that the price of four water bottles is less than the cost of a cook stove plus a pair of boots.

Is the above expression (4w < c + b) true?

SALE!
CAMPING SUPPLIES

t	tents	$200
s	sleeping bag	$180
b	boots	$160
p	pack	$240
c	cook stove	$32
f	frying pan	$18
w	water bottle	$6

Circle the expression to match each group of words below. Then evaluate the expression.

1. cost of three water bottles and two packs:

   3w + 2p   3(w + p)   (3w) (2p)

2. four times the cost of four frying pans and one sleeping bag:

   4(f + s)   4(4f + s)   4(f + s)

3. ten dollars more than two cook stoves:

   c + 2s + 10   10 – 2c   2c + 10

4. cost of three pairs of boots less three dollars:

   3b + 3   3b – 3   b – 3   b + 3

5. cost of a frying pan is less than the cost of two tents

   f > t   2f < 2t   2f < 2t   f < 2t

6. three times the cost of the sum of a pack and boots:

   3p + b   3(p + b)   (3p) (3 b)

7. half the cost of five water bottles:

   (5–2)w   5w + b   5w + 2 $\frac{5w}{2}$

8. the cost of a cook stove, two water bottles, and a frying pan is less than one hundred dollars

   c + 2 w + f < 100   (100 – 2)   (c + 2w + f) < 100

Name

BEAR INVASION

Bears have invaded the campsite (on several occasions!).

Evaluate these expressions to find out about the damage.

	Situation	Expression	Value of Variable(s)	Evaluate the Expression
1	Amount of chocolate the bear ate	$12c + 4$	$c = 4$ oz	
2	Amount of trail mix the bear ate	$t(9 + 11) - t^2$	$t = 4$ g	
3	Volume of a cube-shaped pack carried off by the bear	$V = s^3$	$s = 60$ cm	
4	Area of top surface of sleeping bag bear destroyed (length is three times width)	$A = lw$	$w = 3$ ft	
5	Number of visits from bears	$x(x^2 + 11)$	$x = 2$	
6	Number of snacks in each backpack	$8(2s + 4) - 7$	$s = 6$	
7	Area of tarp shredded by bears (width = 2 m)	$A = lw$	$l = 3$ m	
8	Hours bears spent rummaging in packs	$10h + (h - 4)$	$h = 0.6$ hr	
9	Amount of energy drink the bear drank	$(d)(12)\left(\frac{3}{4}\right)$	$d = 3.4$ l (liters)	
10	Distance bear dragged Mike's pack	$\frac{120d}{3}$	$d = \frac{2}{5}$ yd	

Evaluate the expressions.

11. $x(-6 + 2x)$ with $x = 2$

12. $n + \left(\frac{15n}{3}\right)$ with $n = 3$

13. $(3b)(5d)$ with $b = 4$ and $d = -2$

Name

Common Core Reinforcement Activities — 6th Grade Math

SIMPLY FOLLOW THE TRAIL

Today's trip takes the energetic hikers a long way through the Mt. Blister Wilderness Area. The expressions on the chart represent the distances between places along the trail. On the two days, they followed the trail from the trailhead to Horsefly Pond.

This expression represents the morning hike.

$$x + y + 2.5y + 2x + 0.3$$

To simplify an expression, write an equivalent expression. You can do this by combining like terms. The above expression, simplified, is

$$3x + 3.5y + 0.3$$

Simplify the following expressions.

1. $3a + 5a$

2. $(6x + 2) + (x - 8)$

3. $14k - 6k$

4. $6(c + 3) - 12$

5. $\frac{24n}{6} + 3n$

Write, simplify, and evaluate an expression to solve the problems.

6. On the third day, the hikers traveled from Horsefly Pond past the Fire Lookout to Moose Lake. If $x = 0.5$ km and $y = 1.5$ km, how far did they hike?

7. On the final day, the hikers followed the trail from Moose Lake past Bear Cave to the top of Mt. Blister. If $x = 0.5$ km, $y = 1.5$ km, and $z = 0.8$ km, how far did they hike?

8. On the following day, they returned from the Mt. Blister Summit to the trailhead by the same trail. How long was the return hike? ($x = 0.5$ km, $y = 1.5$ km, and $z = 0.8$ km.)

DISTANCES
(kilometers)

Trail Head to Bear Paw Pond
x

Bear Paw Pond to Lake Achoo
y

Lake Achoo (south end) to Horsefly Pond
2.5y + 2x + 0.3

Horsefly Pond to Fire Lookout
4x + 2

Fire Lookout to Moose Lake
y + 0.6

Moose Lake to Bear Cave
z

Bear Cave to Mt. Blister Summit
2x + y + z

Name

I'm so dry!

Basha

WHERE'S THE WATER?

Examples of Properties
Identify Properties $a + 0 = a$ and $(a)(1) = a$
Zero Property $(a)(0) = 0$
Commutative Properties
        $a + b = b + a$ and $(a)(b) = (b)(a)$
Distributive Property $(a)(bc) = (ab)(c)$
Associative Properties
$(a + b) + c = a + (b + c)$ and $(ab)(c) = (a)(bc)$
Opposite Properties Dividing a number is the opposite of multiplying by that number. Subtracting a number is the opposite of adding that number.

On a hot, dusty trail, the hikers take out their water bottles. They have seven water bottles—all empty. When they calculate how much water they have, they come up with ZERO. That's because seven times nothing (zero) is ZERO. (It's also because they forgot to fill those bottles.) The zero property for multiplication describes what happened to the thirsty climbers. The product of any number and zero is zero.

These other properties of numbers and operations will help you write equivalent expressions when you simplify or evaluate expressions.

Write the name of the property used to create each equivalent expression.

1. $(-40)(1) = -40$ Property:

2. $-x + (y + z) = (-x + y) + z$ Property:

3. $(x + y)(x - y) = (x - y)(x + y)$ Property:

4. $-9 + 9 = 0$ Property:

5. $4(2 + 10) = (4)(2) + (4)(10)$ Property:

6. $x(2x + y) = 2x^2 + xy$ Property:

Use one or more of the properties to create an equivalent expression.

7. $10(2p + q)$ _____

8. $b(3b - 15)$ _____

9. $1(c + d) + 0(c + 4d)$ _____

10. $12g + 9(g - 20)$ _____

11. $2(25n + 13n)$ _____

12. $8c(5c)$ _____

13. $9x^2 - x(x + 5) + 2$ _____

14. $\frac{45p}{9p}$ _____

Name

WHERE'S THE CHOCOLATE?

Basha is doing some calculations about the many chocolate bars she brought along on the hike. Her list tells how many she's borrowed, eaten, melted, lost, or given away. However, she's not exactly sure about some of the numbers.

Circle an answer for each question.

1. Which expression represents the total number of chocolate bars she could have eaten if she had not lost, melted, given away, or had any eaten by bears?

   a. $n + b$

   b. $n - 3$

   c. $(n + b) - 3$

2. Which expression represents the number she lost or melted?

   a. $(n - b) - (x + 2)$

   b. $n - (x + 2)$

   c. $x + 2$

3. Which expression represents the bars she had in her possession at one time but were not eaten by bears?

   a. $(n + b) - y$

   b. $(n + b) - (3 + y)$

   c. $n - (4 + 2 + x + z + b)$

4. Which expression represents the number given away, lost, or eaten by someone other than Basha?

   a. $z + y$

   b. $4 + x + y$

   c. $n - 3$

5. If $n = 25$, $b = 4$, and $x = 2$, what is the number of bars in question 2?

CHOCOLATE BARS

Started with   n
Gave away   4
Melted by fire   2
Borrowed from others   b
Lost   x
Basha ate   z
Still have   3
Eaten by bears   y

Simplify and evaluate each expression using the values for the variables shown in #5.

6. $3(y + 8) - 4$

7. $x + z^2 - z + x$

8. $b(b + y) - n$

Name

EXPRESSIONS ADRIFT

A key skill in solving equations is being able to recognize and write equivalent expressions. There are many expressions adrift in the river (along with the rafter)!

In the water, find pairs of expressions that name the same number (no matter what value is substituted for the variable or variables). Write these pairs on the lines below.

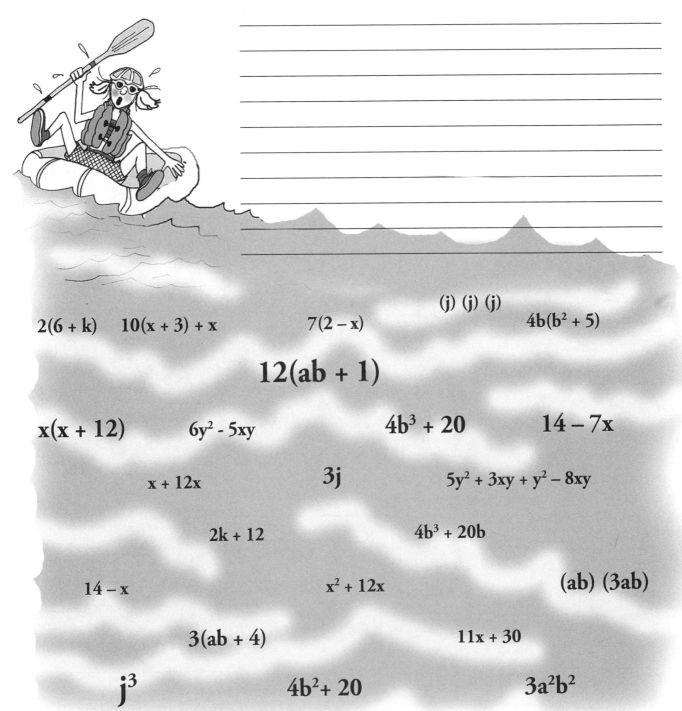

$2(6 + k)$ $10(x + 3) + x$ $7(2 - x)$ (j) (j) (j) $4b(b^2 + 5)$

$12(ab + 1)$

$x(x + 12)$ $6y^2 - 5xy$ $4b^3 + 20$ $14 - 7x$

$x + 12x$ $3j$ $5y^2 + 3xy + y^2 - 8xy$

$2k + 12$ $4b^3 + 20b$

$14 - x$ $x^2 + 12x$ (ab) (3ab)

$3(ab + 4)$ $11x + 30$

j^3 $4b^2 + 20$ $3a^2b^2$

MAKING TRACKS

While wandering through a cave, Chad came face to face with the creature who called the cave "home." Chad retreated quickly, following a path of equations and inequalities with correct solutions.

Find the path Chad followed as he escaped from the cave. For each problem, test the solution value to see if it is correct. If a solution is correct, color the box. Connect the colored boxes to show his path.

A. $3y + 13 = -20$
    $y = -11$

B. $5p - 4 = 31$
    $p = -7$

C. $200 = n + 310$
    $n = -110$

D. $-7r = 84$
    $r = -12$

E. $-2 + 8w = 30$
    $w = 4$

F. $3.6 + -7 = y$
    $-3.4 = y$

G. $5 + 3q = 50$
    $q = 15$

H. $s + 2s = -42$
    $s = 14$

I. $8(c - 4) = -16$
    $c = 2$

J. $8(c + 2) > 16$
    $c = 0$

K. $g = 2(10 - 4)$
    $g = 16$

L. $x + -2 = 33$
    $x = 35$

N. $3(x + 6) = 78$
    $x = 20$

M. $s + 12 < 4$
    $s = 8$

O. $-8m + 2 = 482$
    $m = -60$

Name

CONFUSION AT THE CROSSROADS

"How much farther beyond Razor Rock is Ripple Creek?" Toni wonders. She's standing at the junction of many paths, trying to calculate some hiking distances.

Examine Toni's equations to see if they are true. Use the distances and their matching variables on the signs. (For example, the value of the variable *a* shown on the Achoo Lake sign is 5.) Write *yes* or *no* to tell if she used the correct values to write true equations.

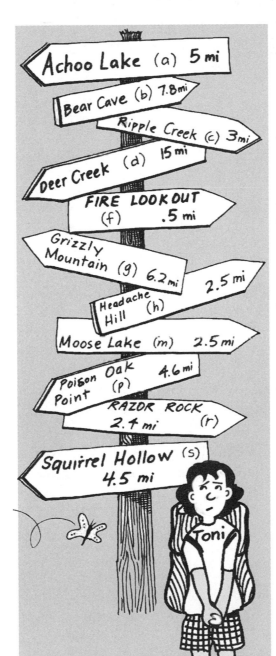

_____ A. a = 2h

_____ B. c − r + f = 1.1

_____ C. $\frac{s}{10}$ = 0.45

_____ D. 2c + 4 = 10

_____ E. 2(d + 1.5) = g

_____ F. b + g − 3 = 8.2

_____ G. m + f + 1.6 = p

_____ H. a + s = c + d

_____ I. g = 2c − 0.02

_____ J. h − f = −2

_____ K. b = 2(r + 3)

_____ L. b − g = 1.6

_____ M. s + 2d = b

_____ N. d = p − a

_____ O. 2s − f = 8.5

_____ P. f + d − c = a − 4

Signpost labels:
- Achoo Lake (a) 5 mi
- Bear Cave (b) 7.8 mi
- Ripple Creek (c) 3 mi
- Deer Creek (d) 15 mi
- FIRE LOOKOUT (f) .5 mi
- Grizzly Mountain (g) 6.2 mi
- Headache Hill (h) 2.5 mi
- Moose Lake (m) 2.5 mi
- Poison Oak Point (p) 4.6 mi
- RAZOR ROCK 2.4 mi (r)
- Squirrel Hollow (s) 4.5 mi

Name _____

Common Core Reinforcement Activities — 6th Grade Math

TO BUILD A FIRE

If there's going to be a good fire on a cold night, everyone needs to help collect the firewood. It looks as if Yolanda may have gathered the most—67 logs! This is 7 more than 4 times as many logs as the rest of the campers combined.

This equation can be used to find the number of logs gathered by the others (n).

$$67 = 4n + 7$$

Write an equation to answer the question for each of these firewood situations. Use a variable to represent the missing value.

1. Zoey collected 32 logs. This was twice Chad's amount. How many did Chad collect (c)?

2. Toni gathered 27 logs. This was 9 fewer than Matt and Basha collected together. (They each gathered the same number.) How many logs did Matt and Basha each collect (l)?

3. Sam's bundle of logs weighed 16.4 kilograms. This was four times the weight of Toni's bundle (t). How much did Toni's bundle weigh?

4. On five days, Monday through Friday, the group collected a total of 86 logs. By the end of the day on Friday, all these were burned. 67 of those burned the first four days. How many logs were burned on Friday (f)?

5. Toni, Mike, and Matt carried equal weights of wood. Together, they carried 72 kg. How much did each carry (n)?

6. The temperature by the fire was 95 °F. This was 5 ° hotter than three times the temperature ten meters away from the fire. What was the temperature ten meters away (t)?

Discuss your decisions about equations with some classmates. Be ready to explain how and why you made your choices.

Name

MARSHMALLOW PROBLEMS

On a campout, the best part of the day is sitting around the campfire toasting those creamy, gooey marshmallows. Tonight is no exception, but there are a few problems with the marshmallows.

For each marshmallow problem, circle the equation that would find a solution. Then solve the equation.

1 Critters ate a total of 73 marshmallows from 4 bags. They ate 23 from Sam's bag, 6 from Chad's bag, and 18 from Matt's bag. How many were eaten from Mike's bag (x)?

a. $73 - 4 - 23 - 6 - 18 = x$

b. $x = 23 + 6 + 18$

c. $x = 73 - (23 + 6 + 18)$

Solution: _____

2 The campers toasted a total of 18 marshmallows. Matt ate less than half of these. How many did Matt eat (n)?

a. $n = 18 \div 2$

b. $n < \frac{18}{2}$

c. $n > \frac{18}{2}$

Solution: Sam ate fewer than _____

3 Basha dropped a number of marshmallows into the fire. Matt dropped 4 times as many. Together, they dropped 15. How many did Basha drop (d)?

a. $15 = d - 4$

b. $d = 15 + 4$

c. $15 = d + 4d$

Solution: _____

4 Someone (or something) ate $\frac{1}{2}$ bag of marshmallows every hour for 3 hours. $1\frac{1}{2}$ bags were left. How many bags of marshmallows (m) were there to begin?

a. $m - 3(\frac{1}{2}) = 1\frac{1}{2}$

b. $3m = 1\frac{1}{2}$

c. $\frac{1}{2}m = 1\frac{1}{2}$

Solution: _____

5 In the last two nights, 24 marshmallows have been burned. The number burned on Monday is represented by m. The number burned on Tuesday is represented by t. How many burned on Monday?

a. $24 = m$

b. $m = 24 - t$

c. $24 + m = t$

Solve for m if t = 18: _____

6 **Write and solve an equation for this problem.**

The marshmallows cost $1.50 a bag. The campers spent $13.50 on marshmallows. How many bags (b) did they buy?

Name

Common Core Reinforcement Activities — 6th Grade Math

CANOE  CALCULATIONS

The whole time Toni is trudging along the path carrying her canoe, she's thinking about how much farther she has left to walk. Sometimes she even counts steps or seconds. It always seems endless! Help her with some canoe-carrying calculations.

Write an equation that will solve each of the problems. Then find the solutions.

1. Toni has carried the canoe for 14 minutes. The trip should take 21 minutes.
   How much more time (t) does she have to walk?

   Equation: _____

   Solution: _____

2. The canoe weighs 41 pounds less than Toni. She weighs 100 pounds.
   What is the canoe's weight (w)?

   Equation: _____

   Solution: _____

3. The trail is 0.9 kilometers long. She has walked 0.06 kilometers less than half of this distance.
   How far (d) has she walked?

   Equation: _____

   Solution: _____

4. Matt has rested 3 times. Zoey has rested 6 times. Toni has rested twice as many times as Matt and Zoey combined.
   How many times has she rested (r)?

   Equation: _____

   Solution: _____

5. Mike carried his canoe for part of the 50-minute trip. Chad carried Mike's canoe for 33 minutes.
   How many minutes (m) did Mike carry his own canoe?

   Equation: _____

   Solution: _____

6. Toni dropped her canoe 18 times. This was 3 times the number of times Basha dropped hers.
   How many times did Basha drop her canoe (b)?

   Equation: _____

   Solution: _____

7. The canoe weighs 70 pounds. Toni weighs 100 pounds. With her pack and canoe, she weighs 208 pounds.
   How much does the pack weigh (p)?

   Equation: _____

   Solution: _____

Name

ROCKY WATERS

The canoe has been swept backwards through a rocky stretch of the river. Help the paddlers navigate the treacherous waters by solving the equations.

For problems 1-8, solve the equations. For problems 9 and 10, write and solve an equation.

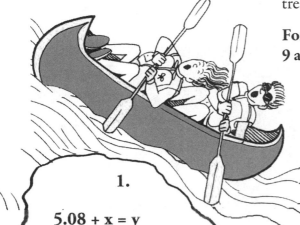

1.

$5.08 + x = y$
$x = 13$
$y =$

2.

$4bc = d$
$b = 10$
$c = \frac{3}{4}$
$d =$

3.

$100m + 40n = 380$
$m = 3$
$n =$

4.

$90.5z = 362$
$z =$

5.

$4k + 87 = 113$
$k =$

6.

$\frac{144}{p} + q = 22$
$q = 10$
$p =$

7.

$1,000 - 7g = 881$
$g =$

8.

$a + 2b = c$
$a = 20$
$c = 86$
$b =$

9.
The water rushed over the rocks at a speed of 3,500 gallons per second. 22,750 gallons rushed over the rocks ahead of the canoe. How much time (t) did this take?

10.
Yolanda paddled 115 strokes as they tried to get past the rocks. Together she and Mike paddled 304 strokes (s). How many strokes did Mike paddle?

Name

Common Core Reinforcement Activities — 6th Grade Math

WITH LIGHTNING ACCURACY

The storm has been raging for hours, and the campers have counted 150 lightning strikes in the last hour alone. To find out how many times lightning has struck per minute on the average, they've used the equation $60t = 150$. Their solution is 2.5 times per minute.

Is this correct? _____

Examine their other solutions. If a solution is accurate, write C on the line. If it is not correct, write the correct solution on the line.

_____ 1. $12x = 72$ $x = 6$

_____ 2. $\frac{n}{25} = 6$ $n = 150$

_____ 3. $4 + p = 27$ $p = 23$

_____ 4. $1{,}250 = \frac{1}{4}q$ $q = 250$

_____ 5. $10k = 360$ $k = 3.6$

_____ 6. $-10.3 = 8.1$ $d = 18.2$

_____ 7. $100 = b + 6$ $b = 94$

_____ 8. $8x = 168$ $x = 21$

_____ 9. $189 = 21r$ $r = 9$

_____ 10. $\frac{3}{4}a = 48$ $a = 64$

_____ 11. The campers bailed out 3.5 liters of water from their tent. Of this, 1.7 liters had seeped through the front flap. The rest dripped through holes in the roof. How much water (w) came through the roof?

$3.5 - w = 1.7$ $w = 2.2\ l$

_____ 12. They timed the duration of thunder rolls. Four thunder rolls in a row were exactly the same duration, with a total of 62 seconds. How long did each thunder roll last (r)?

$4r = 62$ $r = 15.5\ sec$

_____ 13. With the wild storm, the 5 campers got little sleep. They all slept the same amount of time each night. Together, they got a total of 17.5 hours of sleep. How long did each camper sleep (t)?

$17.5 = 5t$ $t = 3.25\ hr$

Name _____

CULINARY MATTERS

Dig your fork (or your calculator) into these tasty
problems about camping food.

**Write an equation to find the solution
for each culinary problem.**

1. Mike cooked up 12 pancakes. That's what his eyes told him that his
   stomach wanted. Before long, he left $5\frac{1}{2}$ on his plate.
   How many pancakes (p) did he eat?

2. Zoey ate $7\frac{1}{2}$ pancakes.
   That's 3 more than her stomach needed.
   How many pancakes (p) did her stomach need?

3. Toni ate several energy bars.
   This was 3 fewer than half the number Chad ate.
   Chad ate 16.
   How many energy bars (b) did Toni eat?

4. Matt's two water bottles were each filled with
   32 ounces of water. At the end of the day,
   7 ounces of water were left.
   How much water (w) did he drink?

5. Some critters carried off 27 packages of oatmeal.
   14 were maple sugar flavor. The rest were blueberry flavor.
   How many blueberry packages (b) were carried away?

6. Sam and Yolanda left a total of 18 chocolate bars in the sun.
   They all melted. Yolanda left a number twice the number of Sam.
   How many of Sam's bars (b) melted?

7. Sam brought 4 times as much stew as Basha.
   Together, they carried 2,990 grams of stew.
   How much stew (s) did Basha carry?

Name

Common Core Reinforcement Activities — 6th Grade Math

PUDDLE PUZZLER

It has rained for seven hours. The puddles are gathering in all the tents. If 1.75 inches of rain have fallen in that time, how many inches have fallen per hour?_____

The equation **11.75 = 7x** will help to find the amount.

Solve the rest of the equations to finish the puzzle.

Across

A. $x + 100 = 146$

E. $\frac{n}{3} = 9$

G. $2{,}200 - g = 89$

H. $p + 3{,}000 = 10{,}000$

I. $2q = 128$

J. $z + 6 = 35$

L. $\frac{m}{3} = 4$

M. $2r = 1{,}850$

P. $k - 5 = 55{,}000$

R. $\frac{s}{3} = 33$

S. $4p = 84$

T. $2t = 98$

U. $g + 92 = 400$

V. $120 = x + 9$

X. $\frac{r}{7} = 9$

Y. $2004 = \frac{p}{2}$

Z. $5f = 75$

BB. $400 - k = 25$

EE. $2q = 130$

FF. $\frac{176}{11} = w$

GG. $x + x = 128$

Down

B. $1{,}000 - g = 400$

C. $\frac{n}{9} = 9$

D. $500 - p = 184$

F. $y - 36 = 36$

G. $\frac{s}{2} = 101$

H. $107 = \frac{n}{7}$

K. $10{,}000 - 480 = d$

L. $5c = 75{,}050$

N. $140 + 159 = g$

O. $100 - w = 41$

Q. $2p = 1{,}036$

T. $\frac{t}{4} = 1{,}029$

U. $999 = 3f$

V. $2{,}000 - r = 994$

W. $63 = \frac{n}{3}$

AA. $11z = 605$

CC. $113 - 42 = b$

DD. $a + 14 = 70$

Name

GHOSTLY INEQUALITIES

Basha told a ghost story. It went on for 45 minutes. Matt told a story, too.
His was not as long as Basha's. This inequality describes Matt's story: **x < 45 and > 0.**
There are several possible solutions. 48 and –5 would not be solutions.

< means *less than*

> means *greater than*

≤ means *less than or equal to*

≥ means *greater than or equal to*

For each inequality, circle the numbers that are solutions.

1. $x \geq 4$	6	-4	4	-2	0
2. $x \leq -1$	4	2	-1	14	6
3. $x > -8$	-8	-10	-6	-2	7
4. $x + 4 < 9$	8	5	-5	3	-2
5. $4x > -12$	-12	6	-3	-5	0
6. $x - 4 \geq 7$	11	-4	6	9	10
7. $\frac{x}{2} < 2$	4	-4	3	9	–6
8. $3x > -9$	-4	-3	3	-2	0
9. $\frac{x}{4} < 8$	7	16	20	-5	60
10. $4x + 2 \leq 7$	2	-1	3	-4	-6

Write an inequality for each of these. Use x as the variable.

11. A number is increased by 10.
The result is greater than 18.

12. 6 is added to 3 times a number.
The result is less than or equal to 2.

Name

Common Core Reinforcement Activities — 6th Grade Math

NOISES IN THE NIGHT

Yolanda and Zoey lost count of all the noises they heard in the night. Zoey heard at least 20. Yolanda knows she heard more. This inequality represents the number she heard:

x > 20

The graph on the number line pictures the solutions for this inequality.

The open circle symbol at 20 shows that 20 is not included in the possible solutions.

This graph shows the solutions to the inequality **x − 3 ≤ 2.**

The solid circle at 5 means that 5 is a possible solution.

Write the inequality shown by each graph.

1.

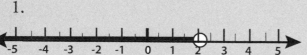

2.

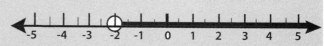

3.

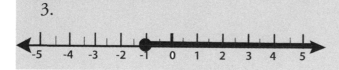

4.

Draw a number line graph showing the solutions for each inequality.

5.   x ≤ -1

6.   x ≥ -3

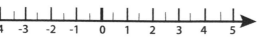

7.   x > -4

8.   x < 5

Name

POISON IVY PROBLEMS

Chad and Zoey are covered with poison ivy. Chad has five times as many spots as Zoey. How many does Chad have? The answer is dependent on the number of Zoey's spots. The equation that represents this problem is **y = 5x** (x for Zoey; y for Chad).

This problem has two variables—one independent, and one dependent. The second one (y) depends on the first one (x).

Complete Table A to show some possible solutions.
Complete Tables B-E to show possible solutions for the equations.
Start by deciding which variable is dependent.

A. y = 5x

x	y	(x, y)
12	60	(12, 60)
10		
8		
6		
4		
2		

B. x + 5 = y

x	y	(x, y)
-3	2	(-3, 2)
-1		
0		
1		
2		
3		

C. x = 2y

x	y	(x, y)
4	2	(4, 2)
-2		
0		
2		
4		
6		

D. x = 3y − 2

x	y	(x, y)
-8	-2	(-8, -2)
	-1	
	0	
	1	
	2	
	3	

E. 3x = y

x	y	(x, y)
-5	-15	(-5, -15)
-3		
-1		
0		
2		
5		

Name

Common Core Reinforcement Activities — 6th Grade Math

LINEAR CONTEMPLATIONS

Mike has had no bites for hours, so he's fallen asleep contemplating the possibilities for his fishing line. Which hook in the graph is attached to Mike's line? You can find out by plotting pairs of variables and drawing a line through them.

y = x + 2		
x	*y*	*(x, y)*
-4	-2	(-4, -2)
-3	-1	(-3, -1)
-2	0	(-2, 0)
-1	1	(-1, 1)
0	3	(0, 3)
1	3	(1, 3)

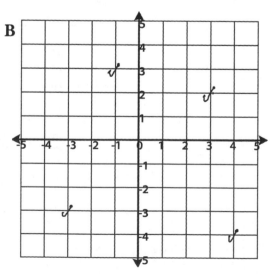

Graph the solutions shown on this table. Draw a line that connects them. This will show which hook is attached to Mike's fishing line.

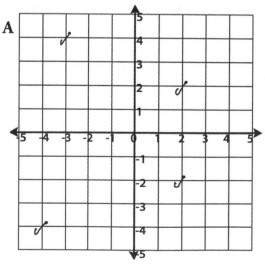

A

y = 2x + 4		
x	*y*	*(x, y)*
-4	-4	(-4,-4)
-3		
-2		
-1		
0		
1		

B

x = -y		
x	*y*	*(x, y)*
-3	3	(-3, 3)
-2		
1		
2		
3		
4		

In Tables A through F on this page and on the next, each table shows an equation. The value of one variable depends on the value of the other. Complete the tables. Graph each solution to find the right hook for the line.

A

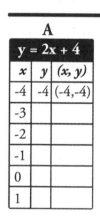

An equation with solutions that form a straight line is called a linear equation.

B

Two-Variable Equations

Graph each "fishing line" equation. Draw a hook at the lower end.

C.   y = 2x
Finish these ordered pairs.
Then graph the solution.

(-2, -4); (0, _____); (1, _____); (2, 4)

D.   y = -2x + 1
Finish these ordered pairs. Then
graph the solution.

(-1, 3); (0, _____); (1, _____); (2, _____)

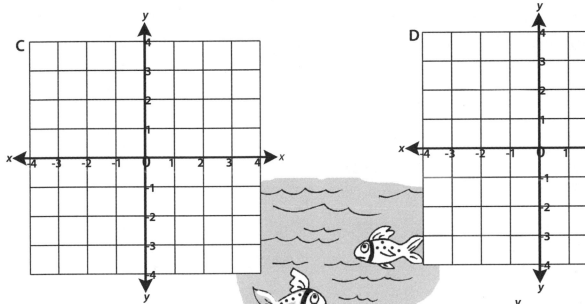

E. y = x + 5
Finish these ordered pairs.
Then graph the solution.

(-4, 1); (-3, _____); (-2, _____); (-1, _____)

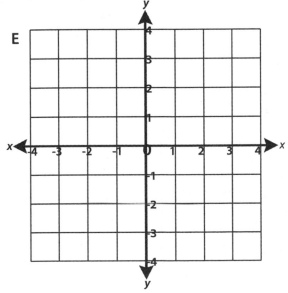

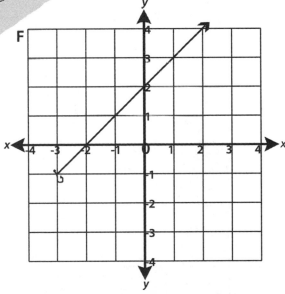

F. Which equation matches this graph?

a. y = x – 1   d. y = x + 1

b. y = 2x   e. y = 2x + 2

c. x + 2 = y   f. 3x = y

SCRAPES, BUMPS, AND BRUISES

The numbers of cuts and scrapes, bruises and bumps, and blisters and bites are growing daily. Together, Basha and Matt have 14 bandaged cuts. How many does each of them have? You cannot find out unless you know the number for one of the campers.

This problem can be solved with an equation that has two variables. One variable will be dependent on the other.

The equation that represents this problem is $x + y = 14$.
(x for Basha; y for Matt)

A

$x + y = 14$		
x	y	(x, y)
2		
4		
5		
8		
10		
12		

Complete the table to show some possible solutions.

1. If Basha has 7, what number does Matt have?

2. If Matt has 3, how many does Basha have?

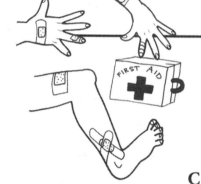

Complete Tables B-E to show possible solutions for the equations.

B

$x = y + 3$		
x	y	(x, y)
-5	-8	(-5, -8)
	0	
	-3	
-2		
5		
	-4	

C

$y = -4x$		
x	y	(x, y)
-3	12	(-3, 12)
	-8	
-1		
4		
	20	
7		

D

$2x + y = 3$		
x	y	(x, y)
-5	13	(-5,13)
-3		
-1		
0		
3		
6		

E

$x - 2y = 6$		
x	y	(x, y)
0	-3	(0, -3)
	-1	
	0	
	2	
	4	
	5	

Name

GEOMETRY

Grade 6

The area of the
landing ramp was
smaller than
I anticipated!

WHAT A FIELD!

The football field has some bare patches this weekend. This presents some unique math problems to find areas of the grassy and bare patches. The length of the field is 100 yards. The width is 50 yards.

Find the area of the field. Use that information to find the area of other portions of the field without using area formulas. Explain how you found each answer.

1. Area of the entire field:

2. Area of each grassy right triangle (ABE and BCD):

3. Area of each bare small isosceles triangle (AGF, FGE, BHE, EHD):

4. Area of figure BHEG:

5. Area of figure ABHEF:

6. Area of figure BEDHC:

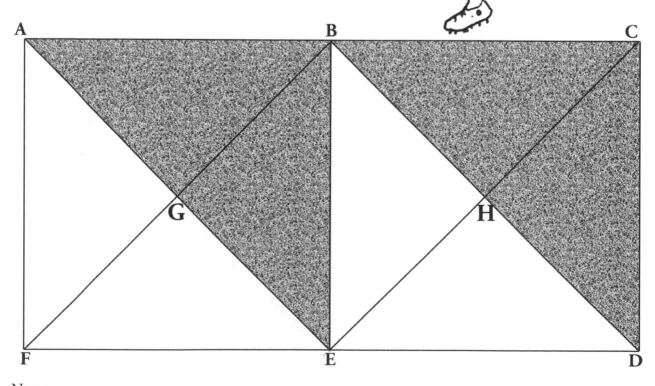

COOL POOL!

Someone got carried away with the repainting of the square pool bottom. The cool design is made up of a great combination of colored areas.

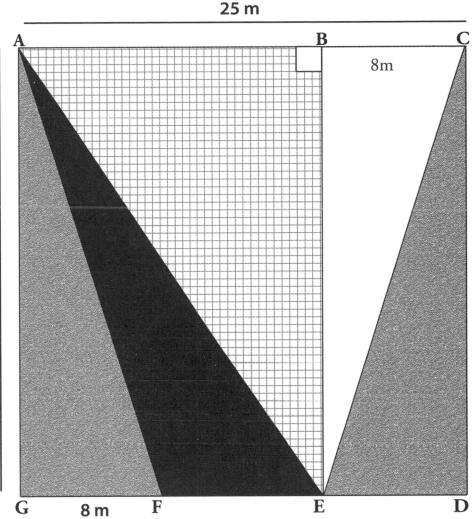

Use the given measurements to determine the following areas. Try to use area formulas as little as possible. Explain how you found each answer.

1. The area of figure ACDG:

2. The area of figure BCDE:

3. The area of figures AFG + CED:

4. The area of figure ACEF:

5. The area of the pool not shaded:

6. The area of figure AEF:

Common Core Reinforcement Activities — 6th Grade Math

POGO PRACTICE

Lucinda has dreams of becoming an extreme pogo jumper. Extreme pogo (or Xpogo) is a sport that involves lots of tricks and jumps on tall, springy pogo sticks. Lucinda will practice on any hard surface she can find.

Here are some of the places Lucinda practices. Solve the area problems by combining shapes or taking them apart.

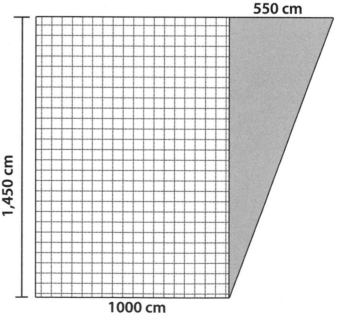

1. Area of the shaded surface:

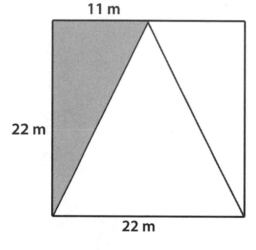

11 m

22 m

22 m

2. Area of the entire surface:

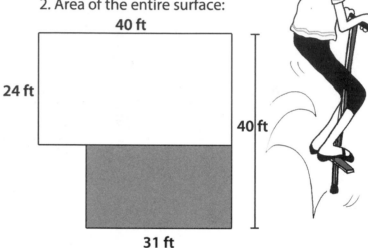

40 ft

24 ft

40 ft

31 ft

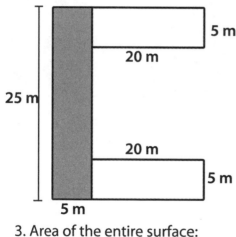

5 m

20 m

25 m

20 m

5 m

5 m

3. Area of the entire surface:

4. Area of the shaded surface:

550 cm

1,450 cm

1000 cm

5. Area of the entire surface:

Name

Use with page 93.

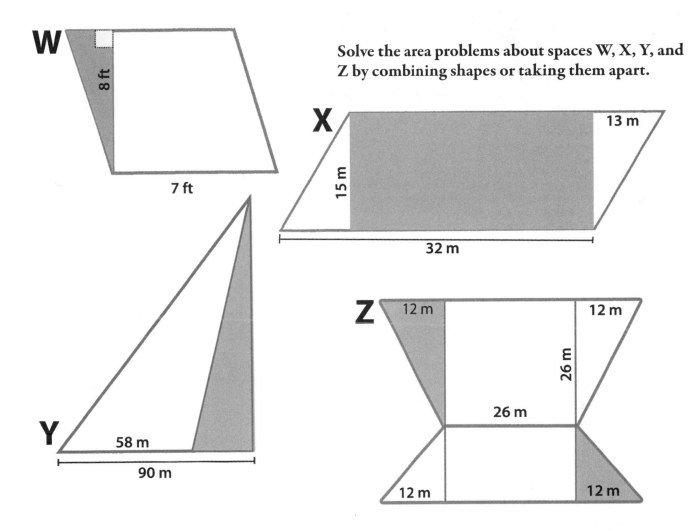

Solve the area problems about spaces W, X, Y, and Z by combining shapes or taking them apart.

6. In figure W (a parallelogram), the base of the shaded right triangle is 2.4 feet. What is the area of the shaded portion?

7. Area of non-shaded portion of parallelogram W:

8. Area of parallelogram X:

9. Area of shaded portion of figure X:

10. Is this true: the area of shaded X > area of non-shaded X?

11. The shaded portion of figure Y (a right triangle) has an area of 1,600 square meters. What is the area of the non-shaded portion?

12. The height of the entire figure Z is 38 meters. What is the area of the lower shaded right triangle in figure Z?

13. Color an area in figure Z that has an area of 312 square meters.

14. Circle the portion with the greater area:

    a. sum of grey-shaded triangles in figure Z
       (Height of figure Z is 38 meters.)

    b. shaded area in figure Y
       (See problem 11.)

Name

Use with page 92.

Common Core Reinforcement Activities — 6th Grade Math

PLACES AND SPACES

The settings where Olympic athletes compete include polygonal places and spaces of all sizes and shapes. Many are quadrilaterals.

Solve these problems about the areas of these spaces.

1. An Olympic speed skating rink has a width of 30 meters and a length of 60 meters. (This is the rectangular size.) If a rink has a diagonal line from opposite corners dividing the rink, what will be the area of each resulting triangle shape?

2. The platform for wrestling can be an 8- by 6-foot rectangle. If the platform's design has a green equilateral triangle in the center with an 8-foot base and a 6-foot height, how much of the platform area will not be green?

3. A 30- by 20-meter water polo pool has a blue bottom surface with a white square shape painted in the middle. The blue portion covers an area of 456 square meters. What is the length of one side of the white square?

4. An Olympic tennis court is a rectangle that measures 78 feet by 36 feet when designed for doubles play. That width is reduced to 27 feet when a singles match is played. See the diagram to the right. If two equal rectangular areas are marked off along the long sides of the court for this change, what is the area of each of those rectangles?

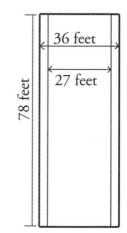

36 feet

27 feet

78 feet

5. Many Olympic wrestling mats are 40-foot squares. If a mat is divided into four equal triangles, with one triangular section red and the others blue, what is the area of the blue space?

6. A regulation Olympic table for table tennis measures 2.74 meters by 1.525 meters. The table is divided into four equal sections for play— with the help of a net halfway across and a painted line that extends down the middle of the length of the table. What is the area of each of those rectangular sections (rounded to the nearest hundredth)?

7. The lanes in Olympic-sized swimming pools can vary. Many pools measure 50 meters by 25 meters. If there are eight lanes of 2.5-meter width in such a pool, how much surface area of the pool is not used by lanes?

Name

THINK INSIDE THE BOX

Volume is the space inside some sort of a container (or three-dimensional figure). Lorenzo wants to find the volume of his box. He can do this by measuring its length, width, and height and applying the formula for volume. Or he can stack it full of identical cubes of a specific unit measure.

Find a small box that has at least one edge with a fractional measurement. Find a large number of measuring cubes or building blocks with an edge that has a fractional measure. Or, use the pattern below to make half-inch cubes. Then compare this to a volume you determine by using the formula A = lwh (length, width, height).

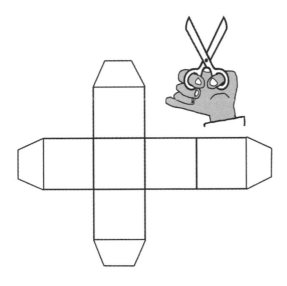

Fill the box with cubes to find the volume.

1. Cubic unit used to measure the volume of the box:

2. Number of cubes needed to fill the box?

Measure the box dimensions and find its volume using the formula A = lwh.

3. Tool and unit used to measure:

4. Measurements:
   length   width   height

5. Apply the formula. Volume =

6. How do the volumes found by the two different methods compare?

Name

HUNGRY FANS

The soccer game has gone into overtime and the fans are hungry! They'll need a lot of snacks before the game is over.

Discover just how much food the fans have. Find the volume or missing measurement for each container. Assume that all the containers are packed full. Then answer questions A and B at the bottom of the page.

1. Maya's popcorn

V = _____

POP'S POPCORN

20.3 cm
15 cm
5 cm

2. Rob's cookies

V = 2,102.5 cm³

height = _____

COOKIES

14.5 cm   10 cm

3. Austin's nacho basket

V = _____

15.5 cm
25 cm   10 cm

4. Joe's crackers

V = 4,132.8 cm³

width = _____

CRACKERS

25.2 cm
20.5 cm

5. Val's taffy

V = 1,530 cm³

width = _____

TAFFY
TAFFY
TAFFY
TAFFY
TAFFY
TAFFY
TAFFY

30.6 cm
5 cm

JUICE in a BOX

14.7 cm
12.2 cm

6. Justin's cheese
(Reduce volume by 400 cm³ due to the holes.)

V = _____

10.5 cm
15 cm   25 cm

7. Lara's drink

V = 1,614.06 cm³

width = _____

A. Which two fans had snacks closest in volume?

B. Which fan had the greatest volume of a snack?

Name _____

Common Core Reinforcement Activities — 6th Grade Math

POOLSIDE PERPLEXITIES

Plenty of prisms can be found in the world of sports. Here are a few examples. Use your volume-finding skills to solve the dilemmas beside the pool and at other sports venues.

Solve the problems to make the perplexities less perplexing.

1. Sara's diving pool needs a minimum volume of $76\frac{1}{8}$ cubic meters for safe diving. This pool measures $12\frac{1}{2}$ meters deep by $7\frac{1}{4}$ meters wide by 10 meters long. Should Sara dive?

2. A container for wet towels is a right rectangular prism with a volume of 25 cubic feet. Each wet towel takes up about $\frac{1}{8}$ cubic foot of space in the container. How many wet towels will it hold if the towels are piled just to the brim?

3. One liter of water has a volume of 0.001 cubic meters. How many liters will be needed to fill a pool that is 20 meters long, 18.9 meters wide, and 4.5 meters deep?

4. Oh, no! Someone left a large container of crackers in the locker room. During swim practice, ants invaded the box. The crackers are gone but the box is packed with wriggling ants. Each cubic centimeter holds 4 ants. The box length is 22.8 centimeters. The width is 10.5 centimeters. The height is 10 centimeters. How many ants are in the box?

5. A giant water cooler on the edge of a soccer field has a width of 0.3 meters, a height of 0.7 meters, and a volume of 0.105 cubic meters. What is its length?

6. A worker at a ping pong ball factory is preparing a shipment. Each ball is securely wrapped and stored in a $3\frac{3}{4}$-inch cubed box. She must fill an order for 120 balls. How would she pack them to fit them into a box that is $34\frac{1}{2}$ inches long, $28\frac{3}{4}$ inches wide, and 15 inches tall?

Name

THE MISSING LABELS

Ms. Wissle, the new athletic director, is confused. New uniforms have arrived for several teams, but all the labels are missing from the boxes. The coaches are asking for their uniforms!

Identify each coach's box from the description given. Complete the missing box letter for all the boxes on this page and the next (page 99).

1.
My box is
1.2 by 1.2 by 2 feet.
Our soccer uniforms are
in box
_____.

2.
The measurements
of my box are
0.4 by 3 by 0.6 feet.
My swimmers'
uniforms are in
box
_____.

3.
Our football uniforms
are in a box that measures
2.8 by 1 by 1.5 feet.
I'm here to pick up
box
_____.

4.
My box has measurements
of 0.3 by 1.2 by 2.5 feet.
The track uniforms are
in box
_____.

A. V = 0.96 ft³

B. V = 1.82 ft³

C. V = 0.9 ft³

D. V = 2.88 ft³

Name

Use with page 99.

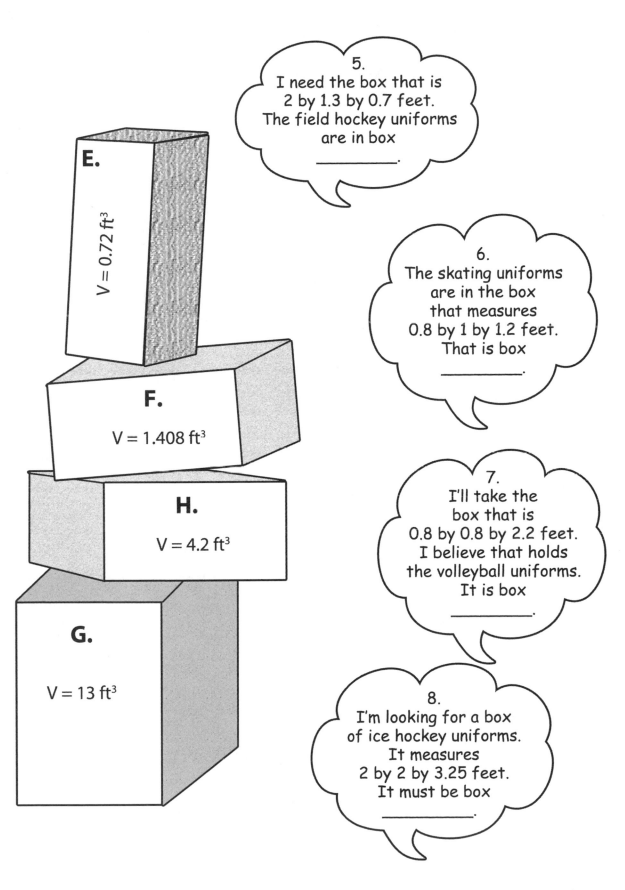

5.
I need the box that is
2 by 1.3 by 0.7 feet.
The field hockey uniforms
are in box
_____.

6.
The skating uniforms
are in the box
that measures
0.8 by 1 by 1.2 feet.
That is box
_____.

7.
I'll take the
box that is
0.8 by 0.8 by 2.2 feet.
I believe that holds
the volleyball uniforms.
It is box
_____.

8.
I'm looking for a box
of ice hockey uniforms.
It measures
2 by 2 by 3.25 feet.
It must be box
_____.

E.
V = 0.72 ft³

F.
V = 1.408 ft³

H.
V = 4.2 ft³

G.
V = 13 ft³

Name

Use with page 98.

Common Core Reinforcement Activities — 6th Grade Math

GEOMETRY ON THE COURT

Things are buzzing on the basketball court.
You'll use it to increase the activity!

**Follow directions on the next page (page 101) to locate
and draw polygons on the coordinate plane.**

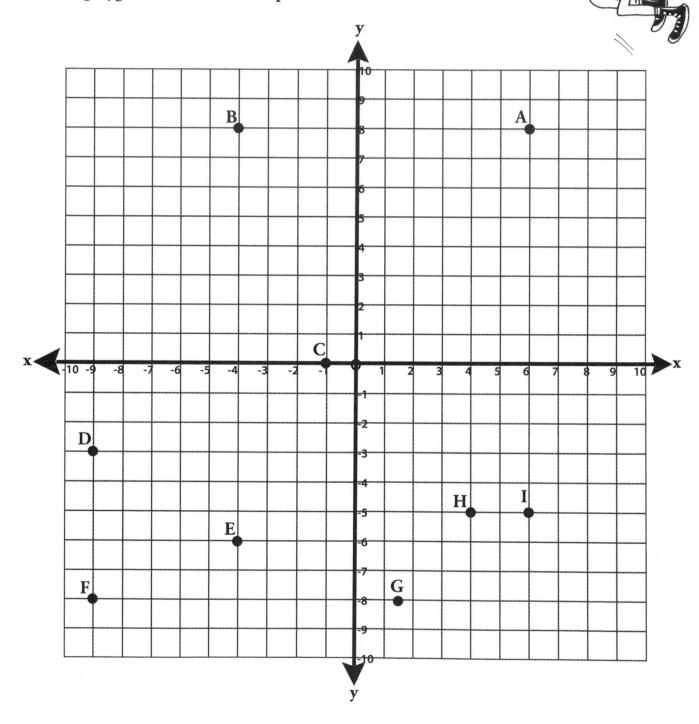

Name

Use with page 101.

Use the coordinate plane on page 100 as you work on these problems.

1. What figure will you draw if you connect points D, E, and F?
   Draw the figure.

2. Give the coordinates of a point that will enable you to draw a regular trapezoid using three existing points.

3. If the edge of each square represents a $\frac{1}{2}$ meter, what is the distance between point A and point I?

4. Draw a parallelogram using points D, E, and C. Label the final vertex J. What is J's location?

5. Plot a point (K) that is a reflection of F across the y-axis. What is its location?

6. Assume that the edge of each square represents a $\frac{1}{2}$ meter. Draw a point that is $7\frac{1}{2}$ meters in vertical distance down from point A. Label this S. What is its location?

7. Draw a polygon XYZ with vertices at (10, -1), (10, -10), and (8, -10). Describe the figure.

8. Plot a point (R) that is a reflection of D across the x-axis. What is its location?

9. Plot the following points. Connect them (in alphabetical order) with straight lines. Connect the final point (Q) back to point L.

L (-2, 6)	O (0, 2)
M (3, 6)	P (0, -1)
N (3, 2)	Q (-2, -1)

   a. Describe the figure you have drawn.

   b. What is its perimeter (assuming that the edge of each square = $\frac{1}{2}$ meter)?

   c. What is its area (assuming each square = $\frac{1}{2}$ meter^2)?

Name _____

Use with page 100.

Common Core Reinforcement Activities — 6th Grade Math

QUIRKY TRICKS

Skateboarders practice tricks with fascinating (and quirky) names—like fakie, ollie, walk the dog, taco flip, and the knuckler.

Use this coordinate plane and the directions on the next page (page 103) to solve some skateboarding problems.

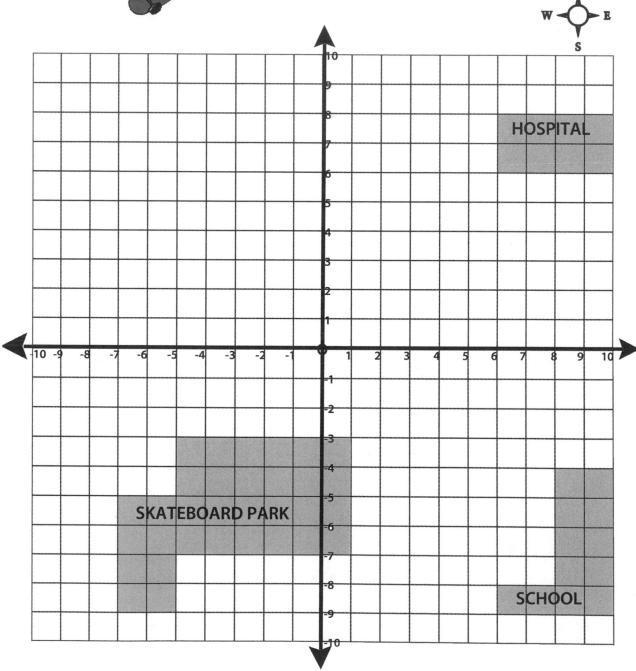

Name

Use with page 103.

Use the coordinate plane on page 102 as you work on these problems.

1. Draw a skateboard silhouette at each point below to show locations of the skaters' homes. Label each home.

Dana (-7, 4) Peyton (2, 6) Amanda (4, -2) J.J. (-1, -10)

2. Assume that the edge of each square represents 0.3 kilometers. How far is Dana's home from the farthest northwest corner of the skateboard park?

3. Assume that each square represents 0.3 kilometers^2. What is the area of the skateboard park?

4. Draw a proposed addition to the skateboard park with coordinates A (-7, -5); B (-10, -5); C (-10, -10); D (-7, -10); and E (-7, -9).

5. What is the area of the proposed addition to the skateboard park? (See problem 4 and use the figure of one square represents 0.3 kilometers^2.)

6. Amanda flies off a ramp, into the air, and out of the park. She takes air at (-4, -5) and lands at a point that is a reflection of that location across the x-axis. Where does she land?

7. J.J. falls off his skateboard on the way to the park at a location of (-1, -8). Using the 0.3 kilometers for the value of each square's edge, how far is it to the southwest corner of the hospital (following only vertical and horizontal lines)?

8. A new skater, Brad, moves into a house at (3, -6). Every weekday, he goes from home to school, to the skateboard park after school, and home. He travels on a straight horizontal path each time. How far does he travel on this path over the course of a 5-day school week? (Assume one square's edge = 0.3 kilometers.)

9. Draw another skateboard park with the coordinates X (-9, -1); Y (-2, 2); and Z (0, 0). Identify the figure created.

Name

Use with page 102.

Common Core Reinforcement Activities — 6th Grade Math

OF FACES, EDGES, AND NETS

Tennis players, badminton players, volleyball players, and hockey players all use nets. Mathematicians use nets, too. A geometry net is the pattern made when a three-dimensional figure is flattened.

Identify the parts of each figure. Envision what a net would look like for each figure.

1.
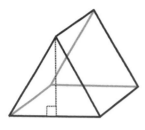
number of edges:
number of faces:
number of bases:
number of vertices:
Color each vertex red.

2.
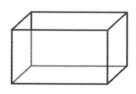
number of edges:
number of faces:
number of bases:
number of vertices:
Color each vertex red.

3.
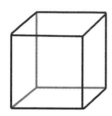
number of edges:
number of faces:
number of bases:
number of vertices:
Color each vertex red.

What happened to my net?

---

4. This is a net of what figure?

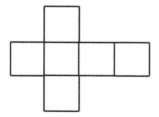

a. a hexagonal pyramid
b. a cube
c. a triangular prism

5. What is the surface area of this figure?
(Each square has 2 cm edges.)

6. This is a net of what figure?

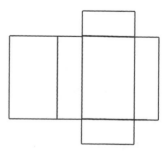

a. a hexagonal pyramid
b. a rectangular prism
c. a triangular prism

Name

Use with page 105.

Reproduce this page and cut out the net. Follow the directions and answer the questions about the figure.

1. Fold forward on the dotted lines. Describe the figure.

2. Find the base or bases and shade it (or them).

3. Trace over edges with red. How many edges?

4. Write a V on each vertex. How many vertices?

5. Unfold the figure and measure the faces (including bases).

6. Find the surface area. S = _____. Explain how you found it.

7. Fold the flaps and tape the figure together.

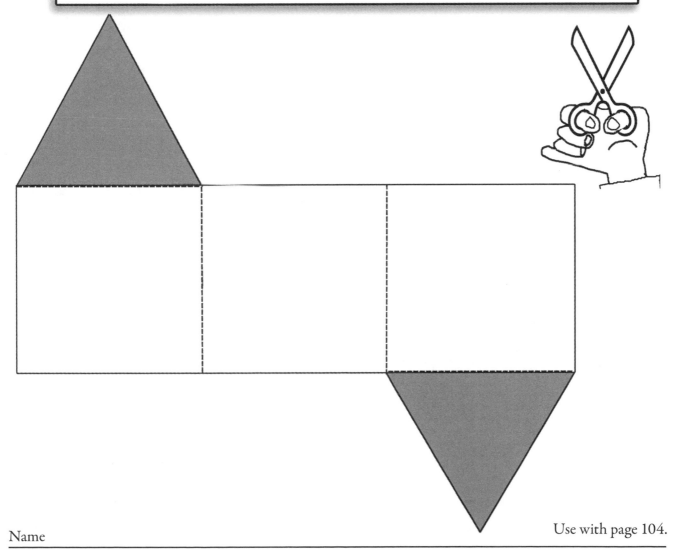

Use with page 104.

Name

Common Core Reinforcement Activities — 6th Grade Math

WHAT STRANGE SPORTS!

People engage in the strangest of sports. New ideas for athletic ventures pop up every day—some of them rather bizarre. This trend does get people moving, and it's usually good, clean fun (except for when it involves garbage, mud, or crawling on the ground!).

Fastest Orange Nose Push

Mike Anderson (USA) pushed an orange with his nose 1 mile in 1 hour and 14 minutes.

1. Alex decided to try the sport of racing on hands and knees while pushing an orange with his nose. He made such a mess of his room (orange juice and peels all over the floor and walls), that it needed some re-painting.

His room measured 6 meters by 7 meters, with wall height of 5.5 meters. He did not paint the ceiling or the door (2.5 meters by 1.2 meters). A liter of paint covered 6 square meters. How many liter-sized cans of paint did he need to buy?

2. Julia and Jane took up racing in a bathtub. The saltwater is hard on the surface of the tub, so they must resurface it inside and out. The tub is a rectangular prism without a top base. It measures 5.5 feet by 2.4 feet by 3 feet tall. Approximately what is the total surface area (inside and out) that they must resurface?

3. Miranda is learning to walk on fire. The fire pit is 0.4 meters deep, 3 meters long, and 1.5 meters wide. Every surface of this rectangular prism is HOT! Find the hot surface area of the pit.

4. Tomas bounces his basketball off the walls, floor, and ceiling while jumping on his mini-trampoline. You can imagine the condition of his room! He will be scrubbing the marks off the entire 15- by 18- by 10-foot prism-shaped room. How much surface area will he scrub?

5. Carlos races garbage cans. His favorite is a cube can with sides of 0.8 meters. It's slimed with garbage on every inside surface, including the lid. How much surface area is garbage covered?

6. Lucy skips rope while brushing her teeth. She keeps a tube of toothpaste handy. It is the shape of a triangular prism with two bases. The triangles have a base of 16 centimeters and height of 6 centimeters. The rectangular faces are 10 centimeters by 20 centimeters. What is the surface area of this container?

Name

106

STATISTICS AND PROBABILITY

Grade 6

Statistically, this was likely to happen eventually!!

ouch!

SPECTACULAR SPINNING

Talented ball spinners have gathered for a competition and a show of their capabilities. The table shows some statistics about their accomplishments.

Lakeside Spinning Competition

	Number of Balls Spun Simultaneously	Duration (in seconds)
Dizzy Al	9	14
Tricky Tess	8	18
Sassy Sue	12	20.5
Cunning Curt	9	17.3
Dazzling Dirk	10	19.6
Amusing Angie	14	31.4

A statistical question assumes variability in the answer (a range of answers rather than one value). Find the statistical questions in these problems.

1. Which of these are statistical questions?
   a. What is the age of the oldest competitor?
   b. How old are the competitors?
   c. How many balls was Sue able to spin simultaneously?
   d. What is the average number of balls spun by the contestants?

2. Which of these are statistical questions?
   a. What is the range of times the six competitors kept the balls spinning?
   b. How long has Sue practiced this sport?
   c. Who spun 50% more balls than Tess?
   d. How long have the competitors been doing this sport?

Answer *yes* or *no* to each question.

_____ 3. Lucy drew four out of six competitors' names out of a box and asked them to rate the location of the competition. Is this a random sample?

_____ 4. Before the competition, a fan polled all the members of Dizzy Al's family to get opinions about who would win the competition. Is this sample likely to be biased?

_____ 5. Blake polled Tess's, Curt's, and Dirk's coaches for opinions about who is the best spinner. Is this a random sample of those who attended the competition?

RECORD BASKETBALL SPINNER

In 1999, Michael Kettman, of the U.S., spun 28 basketballs at the same time. In 2011, he spun 11 basketballs while blindfolded!

Name

DARING DUNKING

SLAM!
Farthest Basketball Slam Dunk from a Trampoline
Thilo Schwarck, of Germany, set this world record in 2012 with a 7.8-meter (25 ft 7 in) shot!

What a great idea to slam-dunk a basketball from a trampoline! The table shows the outcome of the four tries for each player. The winner was the player with the greatest average distance.

Slam-Dunk Distances

Player	1st Try (feet)	2nd Try (feet)	3rd Try (feet)	4th Try (feet)
Stan	10.5	9.8	6.3	6.1
Fran	10	8	11	8.5
Anne	7	7.7	7.2	8.3
Van	12	10.8	9.3	7
Dan	5.2	7.5	8	10.5
Jan	9.2	8.9	9.4	9.5
Nan	14.3	10.5	11	9.9

Answer *yes* or *no* to each question.

_____ 1. Is this a statistical question: Which player had the best second try? (Explain why or why not.)

_____ 2. Luke polled the first 10 fans to arrive at the competition about the importance of this competition.
Is this sample of the total 100 fans likely to be biased?

_____ 3. Brianne polled the five shoppers who spent the most money at the food stand about the quality of the food. Is this a random sample of the 85 customers who bought food at the competition?

_____ 4. Is this a statistical question: How did the second shot for a competitor compare to his or her first try? (Explain why or why not.)

_____ 5. Is this a statistical question: What was the range of distances for the final (4th) shot? (Explain why or why not.)

_____ 6. Is this a statistical question: Which player had the longest slam-dunk distance? (Explain why or why not.)

Name

Common Core Reinforcement Activities — 6th Grade Math

EXTREME SKIING

Some skiers love the thrill of extreme slopes and steep drop-offs. The table on the right shows the number of runs down the mountain for each of many skiers.

Follow the directions below:

A. Transfer the data to the line plot. For each skier, write an X above the mark on the number line showing the number of runs.

B. Describe the data. Tell the number of skiers. Tell what you can learn from the shape of the data on the visual representation.

Number of Ski Runs for Extreme Skiers

9	6	13	10
2	11	10	7
3	7	6	4
10	13	9	11
9	5	5	8
11	11	12	11
4	9	9	6
9	7	10	11
13	10	8	8
5	7	6	3
7	16	5	11
5	11	9	7
10	12	10	12
5	6	8	7
5	8	11	13
10	12	10	15
6	10	10	8
11	11	6	9
8	4	7	10

Ski Run Data

number of runs

Name

THROWING TO GREAT LENGTHS

It seems that people with a competitive spirit will go to great lengths to try to set a record. Here are some of the things people throw in pursuit of zany distance records.

Record-Breaking Throws	
The Farthest . . .	**Approximate Distance** (meters)
Egg Toss (without breaking the egg)	69
Boot Throw	64
Baseball Throw	136
Playing Card Toss	66
Flying Disc Throw	255
Cow Pie Throw	81
Spear Throw	98
Grape Throw	100
Cricket Spit	10

Follow the directions to examine and describe the data.

1. Write the data items in order from least to greatest distances.

2. Circle the number (distance) in the answer to item 1 that falls in the center of the list. (This is the median.)

3. What is the difference between the least and greatest distances? (This is the range.)

4. What is the difference between the least distance and the center distance?

5. What is the difference between the center distance and the greatest distance?

6. What else do you notice about these data?

Name

Common Core Reinforcement Activities — 6th Grade Math

FLIPS, TRICKS, AND FLAT TIRES

In a BMX (bicycle motocross) competition, nothing is quite as exciting as the freestyle and ramp-riding events. Courageous bikers do such wild tricks as spins, flips, rotations, wheelies, and hops. All that action can be hard on tires. Just look at how many went flat during one such event!

Biker	A. J. Ryder	J. R. Crash	Tom Elite	Gabe McTrick	Angie deWheel	B. J. Wynn	Z. Z. Hero	Flip Skyler	Sue Flew
Number of Flat Tires	16	6	14	6	17	3	11	7	9

Answer the questions.

1. What is the *range* of the set of data? (The *range* is the difference between the least and greatest numbers.)

2. What is the *mean* of the set of data? (The *mean* is the sum of the data divided by the number of items.)

3. What is the *median* of the data? (The *median* is the number in the middle when the list is ordered from lowest to highest numbers.)

4. What is the *mode* of the data? (The *mode* is the number that occurs most often.)

5. Which is a number that shows how the values of the data vary: range, mean, median, or mode? (Circle one.)

6. Which summarize a measure of the center for the set of data: range, mean, median, or mode? (Circle all that apply.)

7. The weights of the bikers in kilograms are 43, 40, 49, 52, 44, 41, 41, 48, and 47.

   What is the range?   What is the mean?

   What is the median?   What is the mode?

8. The number of falls for the different bikers was 9, 2, 5, 4, 7, 2, 0, 1, and 6.

   What is the range?   What is the mean?

   What is the median?   What is the mode?

Name

SCRAPES, CUTS, AND BRUISES

The sport of ski jumping is a tale of thrills and spills. Even the best skiers have their shares of falls as they polish their skills. Here is the tale of the injuries during one month of ski-jumping competitions.

Skier	R. C. Snow	C. J. Cool	Todd Rayce	Gayle McTwist	Abby Ariel	Z. Z. Speed	Trip Skyes	Lucy Leep	Sy Sayles
Number of scrapes, cuts, bruises, and sprains	10	6	16	20	13	4	10	8	7

Answer the questions.

1. What is the *range* of the set of data? (The *range* is the difference between the least and greatest numbers.)

2. What is the *mean* of the set of data? (The *mean* is the sum of the data divided by the number of items. Round to the nearest tenth.)

3. What is the *median* of the data? (The *median* is the number in the middle when the list is ordered from lowest to highest numbers.)

4. What is the *mode* of the data? (The *mode* is the number that occurs most often.)

5. The ages of the skiers are 14, 20, 14, 14, 21, 18, 19, 15, and 18.

   What is the range?   What is the mean?

6. The skier that practices the most puts in 18 hours a week. The skier that practices the least practices 11 hours a week. What is the range of this data?

7. The weights of the skiers in kilograms are 38, 41, 40, 39, 40, 46, 42, 38, and 38. C. J. weighs 41 kilograms. Is his weight above or below the median?

8. Gayle weighs 39 kilograms. How far is her weight from the mean weight of all the skiers (including Gayle, herself)?

Name

Common Core Reinforcement Activities — 6th Grade Math

A HUMAN SPIDER

Who would climb a building that is several hundred meters tall? Some adventurous climbers try such feats. They could be called "human spiders!" Scaling buildings is an extreme idea of fun. This climber, Spider Sam Samson, climbed 10 different buildings over the past 11 months.

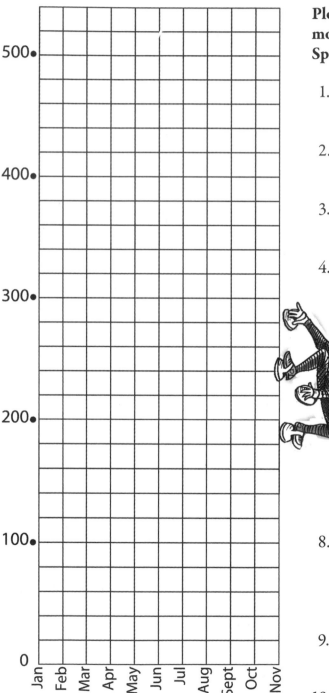

Plot the height of each tower in the correct month. Join the heights with a line to display Spider's climbing data.

1. Spider climbed the 348-meter T & C Tower in Taiwan in the month of April.

2. In July, he climbed the Shanghai World Financial Center, a height of 492 meters.

3. In September, he traveled to Thailand to climb the 304-meter Baiyoke II Tower.

4. South Africa's Carlton Centre, 223 meters tall, was an easy climb in March.

5. In February, Spider scaled the 381-meter Empire State Building in New York City.

6. The Petronas Towers in Malaysia, climbed in June, are 452 meters tall.

7. Spider climbed the 344-meter John Hancock Center in Chicago in August.

8. In May and October, Spider climbed two Australian Towers: the 244-meter Chifley Tower (May) and the 251-meter Rialto Towers (October).

9. In January and November, Spider climbed an 80-meter building in his hometown.

10. Describe the shape of the data.

Name

TAKE OUT THE TRASH!

Yes, people really do race trash cans! If you decide to try the sport, put wheels on the can and don't forget to remove the trash.

Three teams of trash-can racers improve their racing skills in hopes of winning a championship. Every week, they race their cans over a 400-foot-long course. The table shows their practice racing times over a six-week period.

Follow the directions below:

A. Use the graph to display the data from the table. Use a different line (shown in the key) or use a different color to represent each team.

B. Describe the patterns you find in the data.

KEY

Trash Dashers ————————

Rubbish Kings – – – – – – – –

Bin Brigade ·············

SPEED DEMON

Student Norman Schaefer from Germany won the 2012 Garbage-Can Racing World Cup with a time of 21.1 seconds.

time in seconds

| 1 | 2 | 3 | 4 | 5 | 6 |

weeks

Team	Wk 1	Wk 2	Wk 3	Wk 4	Wk 5	Wk 6
Trash Dashers	69	62	50	58	47	45
Rubbish Kings	87	72	66	70	40	55
Bin Brigade	50	45	30	58	72	60

Name

RISKY BUSINESS

High risk accompanies the thrill of extreme sports. Even when athletes use good equipment and follow rules to keep safe, accidents are possible in these dangerous sports. And when the sport takes place high up in the air, mishaps can be even scarier!

One skydiver surveyed 134 friends in the sport to learn about the number of scary mishaps they had experienced. The dot plot shows the results of his survey.

Use the data on the dot plot to answer the questions. Each X represents one skydiver.

1. How many skydivers reported more than 18 scary mishaps?

2. How many more skydivers reported 1 mishap than reported 20 mishaps?

3. Which numbers of scary mishaps occurred with greatest frequency?

4. How many skydivers reported 3 scary mishaps?

5. Compare the number of reports for 4 through 8 total mishaps and
   12 through 16 total mishaps. Circle one answer.
   a. They were the same number.
   b. 4-8 had fewer mishaps.
   c. 4-8 had more mishaps.

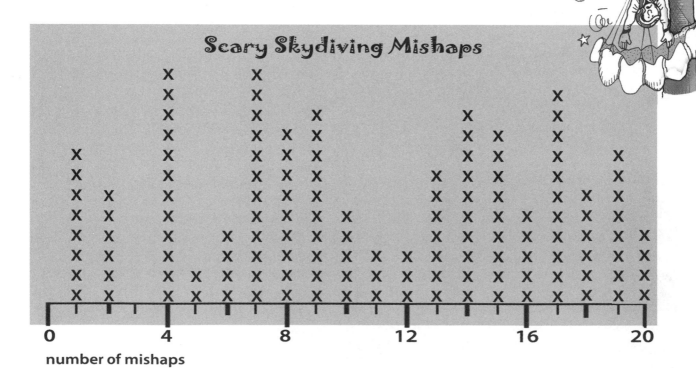

number of mishaps

Name

BUBBLE DATA

The largest bubble blown (without the use of hands) in competition had a 50.8-cm diameter.

Some folks enjoy the sport of blowing bubbles. This may not appear to involve much exercise, but the jaw certainly gets a workout! The table shows some data about the size of bubbles blown in one local school contest.

Follow the directions below:

A. Create a dot plot to display the data from the table.
   Use an X to represent each of the bubbles.

B. How many competitors took part in the contest?

C. What span of five measurements had the most bubbles?

D. Examine the data and the dot plot.
   Describe any patterns you see in the data.

Chad Fell blew that record-breaking bubble in Alabama in 2004.

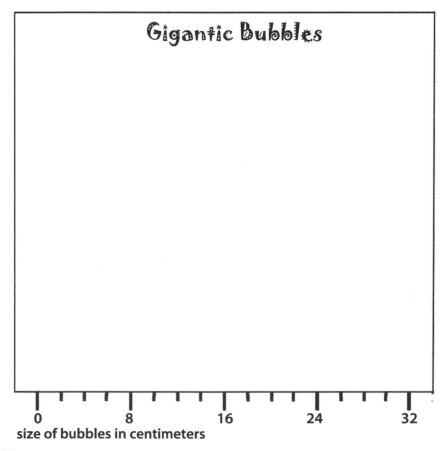

Gigantic Bubbles

size of bubbles in centimeters

0   8   16   24   32

Size of Biggest Bubble Blown for Each Competitor

5	7	13	14
15	10	3	13
18	13	14	15
20	17	17	21
14	14	6	28
9	15	8	29
16	16	16	7
21	17	20	18
22	16	17	16
17	16	15	16
22	31	14	14
13	17	8	15

(in centimeters)

Name

Common Core Reinforcement Activities — 6th Grade Math

AN "EGG"CELLENT SPORT

While the "sport" of egg balancing may not seem to take too much effort, it can take plenty of concentration. The double bar graph here shows two sets of egg-balancing data at once. It shows the performance for five competitors in two different years of competition

Use the data on the graph to answer these questions.

1. Which competitors balanced more than 60 eggs in both years?

2. Which competitors improved from 2013 to 2014?

3. Who balanced a total of about 130 eggs between the two years?

4. Who balanced fewer than 60 eggs in one competition?

5. Who won the 2013 contest?

6. Who won the 2014 contest?

7. Which competitors tied for the second greatest combined scores (for the two years)?

8. Circle letters of any true statements:
   a. More than half the competitors improved their scores from 2013 to 2014.
   b. Rhonda's scores had the least change between the two years.

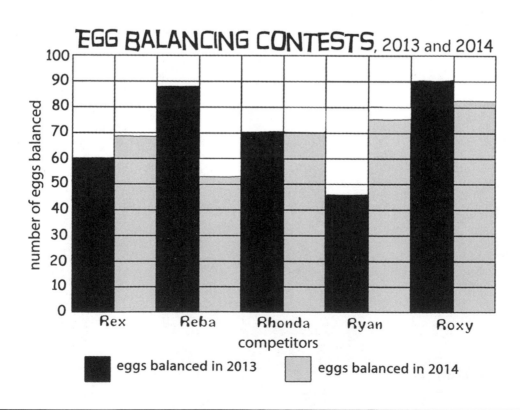

Name _____

ACHES AND PAINS

Injuries are common in many sports, but snowboarding seems to cause many. The table shows the number of injuries at one competition in which a large number of athletes participated.

Follow the directions below:

A. Display the data from the table on a horizontal bar graph. Use contrasting colors for the bars.

B. Describe the data.

Injuries
Snowboard Peak Competition

broken legs	2
broken arms	5
broken noses	3
broken fingers	5
sprained wrists	20
sprained ankles	12
broken teeth	15
pulled ligaments	21
head injuries	2
back injuries	5
bloody noses	19
frostbite	10
sunburn	16

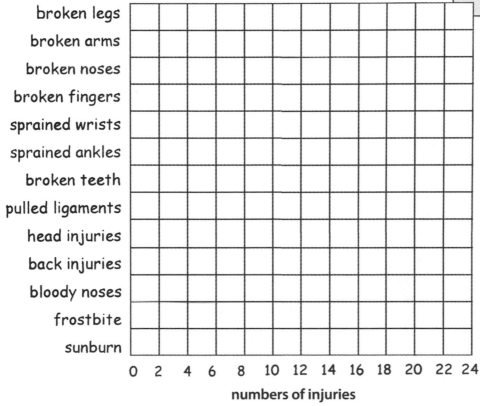

numbers of injuries

Name

Common Core Reinforcement Activities — 6th Grade Math

WINTER EXTREMES

Athletes have been braving extreme weather conditions (blizzards, winds, and cold temperatures) for years to compete in winter sports. Some of the sports themselves are quite extreme—such sports as performing aerial ski tricks, ski jumping, ice climbing, snowboarding, and snowmobile racing. The bar graph shows data about the extreme age differences in a group of competitors at one extreme winter sports competition.

Use the data on the graph to answer the questions. Each bar shows an age span of skiers. The numbers along the side identify frequency with which someone in an age category registered for the competition.

1. Which age group has 28 competitors?

2. Which age groups have fewer than 9?

3. What is the approximate frequency of competitors ages 10-19?

4. Which groups have fewer people than the age 50-54 category?

5. Which 10-year age span has a frequency of about 30 competitors?

6. Which group has a frequency of about 20 more than the 35-39 group?

7. Which groups have a frequency closest to the 10-14 age group?

8. What general observations can you make about the data?

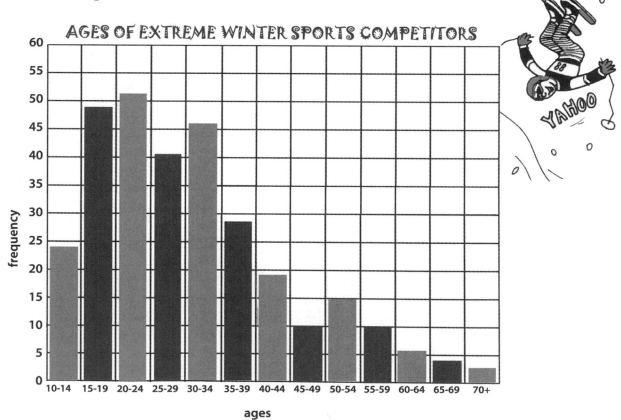

Name

WINTER TRAVELS

Some of the athletes have traveled long distances in the cold winter weather to get to the Extreme Sports Winter Competition. The tally sheet collects the travel frequencies for the competitors by the distances that they traveled.

Use the data on the tally sheet to complete the bar graph. For each mileage category on the graph, color a vertical bar to show the number of athletes traveling those distances. Use contrasting colors for the bars.

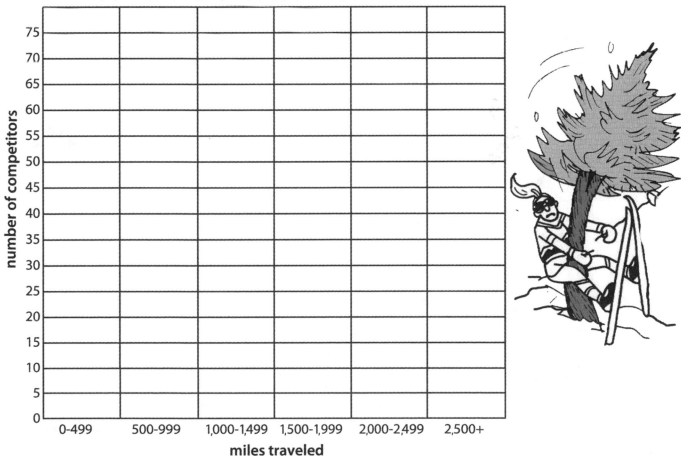

Name

STRANGE TASTES

People eat unusual things on the way to setting records. The quest for championships leads to some rather strange menu items! The graph shows data about some extreme-eating records.

Use the data on the graph to answer the questions.

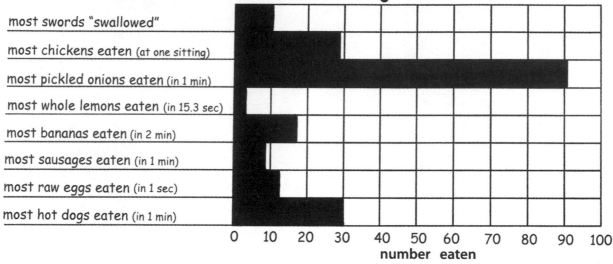

Some Records for Extreme Eating

	0	10	20	30	40	50	60	70	80	90	100
most swords "swallowed"											
most chickens eaten (at one sitting)											
most pickled onions eaten (in 1 min)											
most whole lemons eaten (in 15.3 sec)											
most bananas eaten (in 2 min)											
most sausages eaten (in 1 min)											
most raw eggs eaten (in 1 sec)											
most hot dogs eaten (in 1 min)											

number eaten

1. What has been measured to show this data?

2. What unit is used for the measurement?

3. If the record-holder for lemon eating could continue eating lemons at that same rate for a minute, about how many lemons would be eaten in 1 minute?

4. Which item, if eaten at the same rate for 2 minutes instead of 1, would show about the same number eaten as the record for bananas?

5. Compare the numbers of the items eaten in the specific time periods of two minutes or less. What conclusion can you draw from this information?

6. Describe one other conclusion you could reach from these data about eating one or more of the items.

EW! I thought they meant lemon PIE!

Name _____

ICY STATISTICS

In 2013, a group of 5,834 snowball throwers set a world record for the largest snowball fight. The fight lasted just one and one-half minutes! This mania for snowball fighting is not limited to record-setters. The table shows some data about snowballs another group collected.

Use the data in the table to answer the questions.

1. What has been measured to show this data?

2. What unit is used for the measurement?

3. Over what period of time were the data collected?

4. How do the data change from Monday to Saturday?

5. Jana weighed each of the 10 largest snowballs in the stockpile. Was this a random sample of the total snowballs collected?

6. Sean measured the size of 50 different snowballs drawn at random from the total pile. Was this sample representative of all the snowballs?

7. 14 people from the winning team were asked how they felt about the fight. Was this an unbiased sample?

8. Randy passed out hot chocolate to his 15 friends who were part of the fight. Was this a random sample of all the people who participated?

9. If 40 people took part in the 5-minute snowball fight, each throwing 20 pounds of snowballs a minute, did they run out of snowballs (from the accumulated number shown in the table) and have to scoop up more snow during the fight?

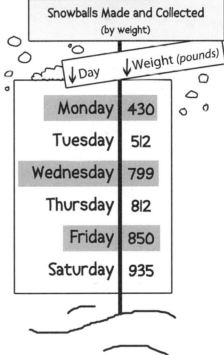

Snowballs Made and Collected
(by weight)

Day	Weight (pounds)
Monday	430
Tuesday	512
Wednesday	799
Thursday	812
Friday	850
Saturday	935

Name

TALL DROPS AND LONG RIDES

Amusement parks around the world keep building steeper, longer, taller, and more thrilling roller coaster rides. The tables below give statistics about some of the world's tallest and longest coasters. A roller coaster-riding club, the Coaster Fanatics, took part in marathon rides on some of the world's longest coasters. The lower table shows data about the hours club members rode over a two-week time period.

Use the data from the tables to answer the questions on page 125. Round answers to the nearest tenth.

Tall Drops

Coaster	Location	Vertical Drop (meters)
Kingda Ka	Jackson, NJ, USA	127
Top Thrill Dragster	Sandusky, OH, USA	120
Superman: Escape from Krypton	Valencia, CA, USA	100
Tower of Terror	Queensland, Australia	100
Steel Dragon	Nagashima, Japan	93
Millennium Force	Sandusky, OH, USA	91
The Titan	Arlington, TX, USA	78

In 2007, American Richard Rodriguez rode a roller coaster for more than 405 hours straight to set a world record. (He was allowed a 5-minute break each hour.)

Long Coasters and Long Rides (by the Coaster Fanatics)

Coaster	Location	Length (meters)	Hours of Riding
Ultimate	Yorkshire, UK	2,268	450
The Beast	Mason, OH, USA	2,243	420
Formula Rossa	Abu Dhabi, UAE	2,200	375
Fujiyama	Yamanashi, Japan	2,045	405
Millennium Force	Sandusky, OH, USA	2,010	390
Voyage	Santa Claus, IN, USA	1,964	355
Vertigorama	Buenos Aires, Argentina	1,816	355

Name

Use with page 125.

Use the data from the tables on page 124 to answer the questions.
Round answers to the nearest whole number.

1. What is the median of the vertical drops?

2. What is the mode of the vertical drops?

3. About how far does the drop of *The Titan* vary from the mean?

4. About how far does the mean (of the vertical drops) vary from the mode and median?

5. What is the range of vertical drops?

6. What is the median of the length of coaster rides? (See bottom table.)

7. How far does the length of the *Voyage* ride vary from the mean of all the coaster lengths?

    Circle one: a. less than 25 m   b. about 85 m   c. more than 100 m

8. How far does the length of the *Ultimate* ride vary from the mean of all the coaster lengths?

    Circle one: a. less than 25 m   b. about 100   c. about 200 m

9. What is the range of hours ridden by members of the Coaster Fanatics Club?

10. What is the mean of the hours ridden? (Round to the nearest tenth.)

11. What is the frequency of a number of hours greater than 400?

12. How far does the statistic on hours ridden on *Formula Rossa* vary from the median?

13. Is the mode the best measure of central tendency to describe the center of the data for hours ridden on the coasters? Explain your answer.

Name _____

Use with page 124.

Common Core Reinforcement Activities — 6th Grade Math

WHAT A RIDE!

You may never take a ride like this, but some adventuresome people actually do fly through the air with the help of a cannon blast. (What better use is there for a cannon?)

Examine some data about this unusual sport to solve the problems below.

> In a human cannonball practice, the following distances were recorded.
> 40 m; 36 m; 41 m; 12 m; 12 m; 12 m; 10 m

1. Which measure of central tendency best represents the center of these data? (Explain your answer.)

2. What is the range of the data?

3. How far is the greatest distance from the median of the data?

4. What is the frequency of distances less than 15 m?

David "The Bullet" Smith, Jr.

In 2011, with a distance of 59.05 meters, Smith set a world record for the longest distance a human was shot from a cannon. He traveled at 120 kilometers per hour.

> In a human cannonball practice, the following heights (in meters) were recorded.
> 4, 6, 6, 3, 3, 3, 1, 4, 7, 19

5. What is the mean of these data?

6. What is the median?

7. What is the mode?

8. Which is the best measure of center?

Explain your answer.

9. What is the range?

10. What is the interquartile range (IQR)?

11. Which is the best measure of variability for these data: range or interquartile range?

Explain your answer.

Name

ASSESSMENT AND ANSWER KEYS

This will be a
test of my skills,
all right!

MATH ASSESSMENT

PART ONE: RATIOS AND PROPORTIONAL RELATIONSHIPS

A total of 50 bulls were brought in for a bullfight. 15 had already fought and been killed in the event, 22 were waiting and ready to go. Another 8 were sick, and 5 more were asleep.

1. What is the ratio of sick bulls to sleeping bulls?

2. What is the ratio of bulls that had already been killed in fights to the bulls waiting?

3. What is the reduced ratio of total bulls to sleeping bulls?

4. Which ratio is greater: waiting bulls to sick bulls or total bulls to sleeping bulls?

5. Martina took a train to the bullfight. It traveled 544 km nonstop in 8.5 hours to get there. If the train moved at a steady speed, what was the rate of travel?

6. Two trains traveled from opposite directions on parallel tracks toward the bullfight town. They started 1,110 km apart at exactly the same time. **Train A**'s speed was 55 km/h and **Train B**'s speed was 85 km/h. Would the trains have met within 5 hours?

7. One bull made 27 charges in 9 minutes. How many charges was this per minute?

8. The total value of the 50 bulls was $800,000. Assuming the bulls were of equal value, what was the value of each bull?

9. At the food bar, Sophia bought a 4-pound bag of peanuts for $1.08. What was the cost per pound?

10. Carlos bought a box of 18 tacos to share with friends. He paid $37.80. What was the price per taco?

11. Matador (bullfighter) Miguel had no injuries in 6 out of his first 15 bullfights. Complete the table with ratios equivalent to this ratio.

Fights with no injuries	6					
Total fights	15					

12. Matador Luis practiced 10 hours fighting real bulls to every 35 hours with a simulated bull. Complete the table with ratios equivalent to this ratio.

Real bullfights	10					
Simulated bullfights	35					

Name

Copyright © 2014 World Book, Inc./
Incentive Publications, Chicago, IL

Each ratio (13-16 below) matches one of the lines on the coordinate plane. Write the letter that names the line.

_____ 13. 15 injuries in 10 fights

_____ 14. 5 injuries in 10 fights

_____ 15. 3 injuries in 5 fights

_____ 16. 12 injuries in 3 fights

17. Draw a line on the plane to represent the ratio of one injury in every ten bullfights. Label the line **E**.

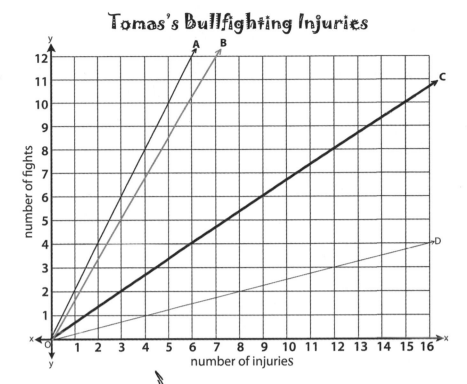

Tomas's Bullfighting Injuries

18. In a crowd of 1,420 spectators, 568 cheered for the matador. The rest cheered for the bull. What percent of the crowd cheered for the bull?

19. During one bullfighting event, 12 bulls were killed. This was 15% of the bulls present for the event. What was the total number of bulls present?

20. A total of 60 matadors participated in the grand finale of an event in Portugal. 55% of these bullfighters were from other countries. How many were from Portugal?

21. The Plaza Mexico arena holds 48,000 spectators. If 31,680 people in the full arena had attended a bullfight before, what percent of the crowd was made up of first-timers?

22. A group of friends in Chicago watched a televised bullfight. They ordered 3 pizzas @ $15 each, 15 drinks @ $1.50 each, and 6 large nachos @ $5.80 each. After adding 5% tax and a 20% tip to the total, what did they pay for the food? (The tip is 20% of the total before the tax is added.) Round the answer to the nearest whole cent.

Name

Copyright © 2014 World Book, Inc./
Incentive Publications, Chicago, IL

PART TWO: THE NUMBER SYSTEM

Organizers of a hot-air balloon race had $1\frac{3}{4}$ large fields prepared for landings. Each balloon needed $\frac{2}{8}$ of that space. Find out how many balloons could land in the prepared area.

1. Draw a box around each $\frac{2}{8}$ section within the shaded area.

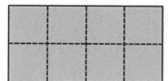 

2. Solve the equation: $1\frac{3}{4} \div \frac{2}{8} =$

Solve the problems.

3. A hot-air balloon owner used 2,240 liters of propane in 28 flights. What was the average amount of fuel used per flight?

4. At one race, officials decided that each balloon needed 8,500 square meters for landing space. How much space was needed to land 13 balloons in their own space at the same time?

5. After a race, some of the competitors shared 22 sandwiches in equal portions. Each had $2\frac{3}{4}$ sandwiches. How many people ate?

6. Which is the correct factorization of **24 + 84 - 36** making use of the greatest common factor?

   a. $8(3 + 1.5 - 4)$
   b. $12(2 + 7 - 3)$
   c. $4(6 + 21 - 6)$

Solve the problems.

7. Balloon-owner Tabitha packs a basket of cheese-and-cracker snacks for her trip. The crackers come in boxes of 12 and the cheese comes in packages of 15 slices. What is the least number of packages of each she must buy in order to make snacks of single slices of cheese on single crackers without any cheese or crackers left over?

8. $|-16| - |16| =$

9. $|5.9| + |-22| =$

10. $|-13| - |7.5| =$

11. Is this true: $|-20| > |19|$?

12. Is this true: $|14| < |-24|$?

13. Is this true: $|0.9| = |-0.9|$?

14. Is this true: $|-6.8| + |6.8| = 0$?

Name

15. What number represents the temperature three degrees below zero Celsius?

16. Which temperature is lower: -18 °C or 16 °C?

17. What temperature is 24 ° warmer than -12 °C?

18. The temperature rose from -6 °C to 49 °C. What was the change?

Use the line graph to answer the questions.

19. Where did balloon X land?

20. Which balloon landed at $\frac{4}{5}$?

21. Where did balloon Y land?

22. Where did balloon S land?

23. Draw a balloon landing at the opposite of -2.8. Label it Z.

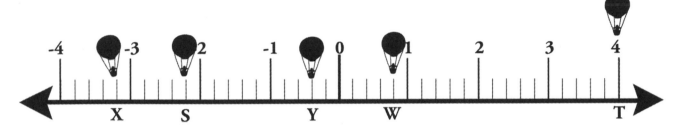

24. Draw and label dots to show balloons landing at these locations:

   A (4, 6)   **E** (4, -3)

   B (-5, 0)   **F** (-7, -6)

   C (-3, -4)   **G** (-3, 7)

   D (0, -7)   **H** (7, -4)

25. What is the distance between C and G (in units)?

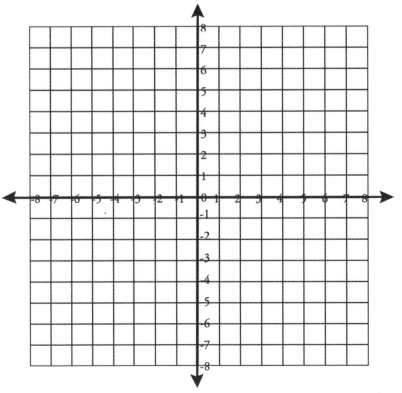

Name

Common Core Reinforcement Activities — 6th Grade Math

PART THREE: EXPRESSIONS AND EQUATIONS

Write an expression to match each statement.

1. twice the finish time (t) plus 5 seconds

2. 10 times the sum of wind speed (s) and wave resistance (w)

3. a distance (d) increased by 3 meters

4. half the sum of a number (n) and twice another number (p)

5. twice the time (t) less 52 seconds

6. -12 times the difference between a number (x) and the square of a second number (y)

Are the expressions equivalent? Write _yes_ or _no_ for each one.

_____ 7. $10 - 12$ $12 - 10$

_____ 8. $5(6 + x^2)$ $30 + 5x^2$

_____ 9. $\frac{84}{4}$ $\frac{42}{2}$

Evaluate the expressions for a = -5 and b = 9.

10. $3(a - b)$

11. $5b^2 + a$

12. $4a + 2b + b^2$

13. $\frac{9a}{b}$

14. $100 - 2a - 10b$

Write and solve an equation for each problem.

15. A water-walking team drank 16 liters of water. A second team drank a different amount. Together, they drank 38.5 liters. How much water did the second team drink (w)?

16. Together, two water-walkers covered 135 meters in practice. Toni walked 3.5 times the distance of Abby. What was Abby's distance (d)?

17. Derek walked a number of strides (s) to get to the finish line. Mariah walked $\frac{3}{4}$ Derek's number. Together they walked 3,500 strides. How many strides did Derek walk?

18. Stefano walked at a rate of 0.4 meters per second. His total walk covered 1,520 meters. How much time (in seconds) this take (t)?

Name

Write the inequality shown by each graph.

19.

20.

Draw a number line graph showing the solutions for each inequality.

21. **x ≤ 4**

22. **x > -2**

23.

Complete the tables to show some solutions for each equation.

x + y = 4		
x	**y**	**(x, y)**
-3		
-2		
-1		
0		
1		
2		

24.

y = 2x		
x	**y**	**(x, y)**
-4		
-2		
0		
2		
4		
6		

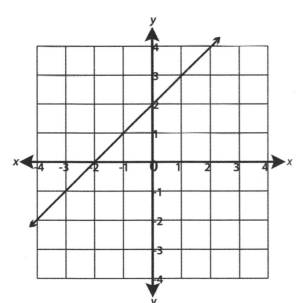

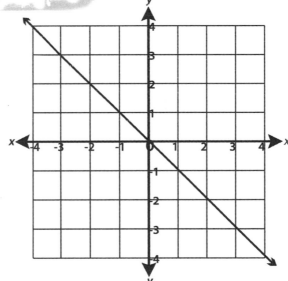

25. Which equation matches the graph?

  a. x = y + 2   c. y = x–2

  b. y = x + 2   d. y = 2x

26. Which equation matches the graph?

  a. x = y   c. y = x – 1

  b. y = x + 2   d. y = -x

Name

Common Core Reinforcement Activities — 6th Grade Math

PART FOUR: GEOMETRY

The skateboard park is a 100- by 50-meter area. The fancy patterns painted on the cement are made of 8 right triangles. Answer 2-5 without using any formulas. Explain how you found each area.

1. Area of the entire park:

2. Area of ABF:

3. Area of FGCH:

4. Area of figure with vertices FCHDE:

5. Area of BCG:

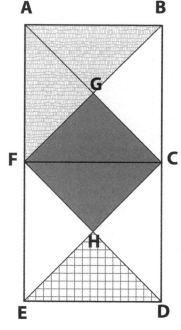

Solve the problems.

6. A triangular skating surface (ABC with a right angle at A) has an area of 7,200 m² and a height of 120 m. What is the measurement of its base?

7. A skating ramp is a 35- by 12-foot rectangle. What is its area?

8. What is the area of the unshaded part of the figure below?

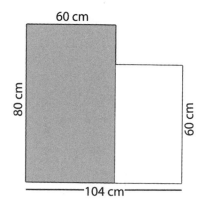

9. Lexi's new skates came in a rectangular-prism-shaped box with a volume of 137,500 cm³. Its height and width were 50 cm each. What is the box's length?

10. A storage shed in her back yard is a great spot for Lexi's skating equipment. The shed (a rectangular prism) is 20 ft long, 9 ft tall, and 14 ft wide. What is its volume?

Name

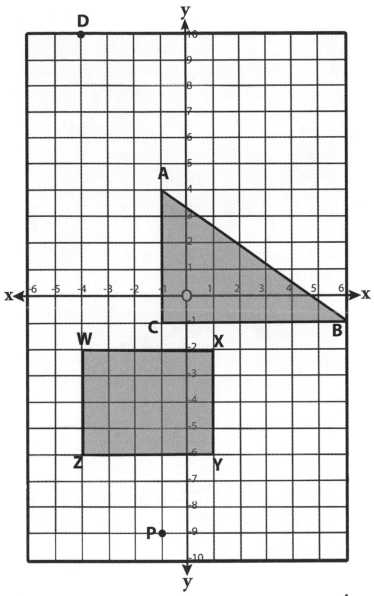

Use the coordinate plane to answer the questions.

11. What is the distance between X and W?

12. What is the distance between D and Z?

13. What is the area of figure ABC (in units)?

14. What is the distance between A and P?

15. If figure WXYZ were reflected over the x-axis, where would point Y be located?

16. If figure ABC were moved 3 units to the left and 4 units up, where would point A be located?

17. What is the area of figure WXYZ?

18. How far is C from B?

Use the figure below to solve problems.

19. The juice box has a volume of 2,200 cm³. What is its width?

20. One cubic centimeter equals 0.001 liter. How many liters would this juice box hold?

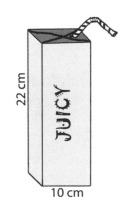

22 cm

JUICY

10 cm

Use the figure below for questions 21 and 22.

21. The image below is a net of what figure?

22. The figure has a length of 10 inches, a height of 4 inches, and a width of 5 inches. What is its surface area?

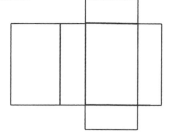

Name

Common Core Reinforcement Activities — 6th Grade Math

PART FIVE: STATISTICS AND PROBABILITY

Circle one or more answers.

1. Which of these are statistical questions?
   a. How many injuries did team members suffer last year?
   b. How many injuries did gymnast Lindsey suffer last year?
   c. What was the range of scores for the balance beam?
   d. What were the scores of the athletes who did not qualify?
   e. How old are the competing skaters?

Answer *yes* or *no*.

_____ 2. Before a speedskating meet, Shana polled members of the first team to arrive to find their opinions about the best skates to buy. Is this sample representative of the 80 skaters at the meet?

_____ 3. Jules chose 30 spectators at random and asked them to name their favorite gymnast at the meet. Is this sample likely to be biased?

_____ 4. Gabe polled the parents of the 12 injured skaters about the safety of the sport. Is this a random sample?

_____ 5. Zack found the ages of 40 of the 80 skaters by choosing every other name on the team rosters. Is this a random sample?

Team Hours of Practice Lost in March Due to Sports Injuries

Team	Spinners	Neons	Lions	Blades	Ringers	Archers	Wizards	Fliers	Bullets
Lost Practice Hours	16	16	12	14	16	15	11	40	13

Use the table above to answer the questions.

6. What is the mean of the data?

7. What is the median of the data?

8. What is the mode of the data?

9. Which measure of center best represents the data? Explain your choice.

10. How far from the mean of the data is the number of hours lost by the Wizards?

11. What is the range of the data?

12. What is the interquartile range of the data?

13. Which measure of variability (from 11 and 12 above) best represents the data? Explain your choice.

14. What is the frequency of times that vary more than 2 hours from the median?

Name _____

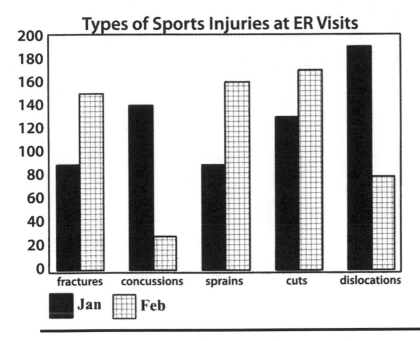

Types of Sports Injuries at ER Visits

Legend: ■ Jan ▦ Feb

Use the data on the graph to answer the questions.

15. Which injury had the greatest change in number between the two months?

16. If the fracture rate trend continues, how many would you expect to see in March?

17. What is the approximate range of the total data?

18. A. Transfer the data on the table to make a line plot. Draw an X to represent each athlete interviewed, placing the X above the number line to represent the number of extreme sports tried by the athlete.

B. Make one observation about the data.

Extreme Sports Tried

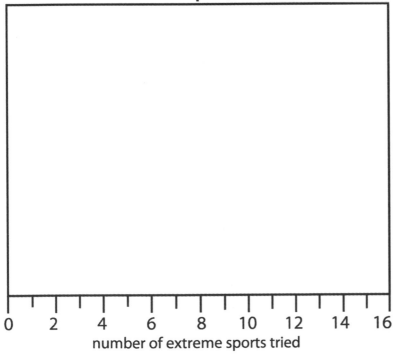

number of extreme sports tried

Number of Extreme Sports Tried by 75 Athletes

1	3	9	3	1
12	15	1	4	5
4	0	8	0	2
0	5	13	0	0
10	2	4	5	6
3	1	8	1	5
8	10	0	10	3
12	5	10	2	0
2	3	3	6	3
9	1	0	7	2
3	2	4	8	1
6	4	3	0	3
1	2	1	5	0
4	7	4	1	8
0	6	2	7	4

Name

Common Core Reinforcement Activities — 6th Grade Math

ASSESSMENT ANSWER KEY

Part One: Ratios and Proportional Relationships

1. 8:5 (or $\frac{8}{5}$ or 8 to 5)
2. 15:22 (or $\frac{15}{22}$ or 15 to 22)
3. 10:1 (or $\frac{10}{1}$ or 10 to 1)
4. total bulls to sleeping bulls
5. 64 km/h
6. no
7. 3
8. $16,000
9. $0.27
10. $2.10
11. Ratios will vary. Check to see that they are
12. Ratios will vary. Check to see that they are
   equivalent to $\frac{6}{15}$.
   equivalent to $\frac{10}{35}$.
13. C
14. A
15. B
16. D
17. Check to see that line passes from zero through (1, 10)
18. 60%
19. 80
20. 27
21. 34%
22. $127.88

Part Two: The Number System

1. Check to see that seven sections ($\frac{2}{8}$ each) have been circled.
2. 7
3. 80 liters
4. 110,500 m²
5. 8
6. b
7. five boxes
   of crackers and four packages of cheese
8. 0
9. 27.9
10. 5.5
11. yes
12. yes
13. yes
14. no
15. -3 °C
16. -18 °C
17. 12 °C
18. 55 °
19. -3$\frac{1}{5}$ (or -3.2)
20. W
21. -$\frac{2}{5}$ (or -0.4)
22. -2$\frac{1}{5}$ (or -2.2)
23. Check for balloon Z drawn at 2.8.
24. Check for points
   labeled A-H at given locations on the plane.
25. 11 units

Part Three: Expressions and Equations

1-6. Expressions may vary. Check for accuracy.
1. 2t + 5
2. 10(s + w)
3. d + 3
4. $\frac{n+2p}{2}$
5. 2t – 52
6. -12(x – y²)
7. no
8. yes
9. yes
10. -42
11. 400
12. 79
13. -5
14. 20
15-18. Equations may vary. Check for accuracy.
15. 16 + w = 38.5; w = 22.5
16. d + 3.5d = 135; d = 30
17. s + $\frac{3}{4}$s = 3,500; s = 2,000
18. 0.4t = 1,520; t = 3,800
19. x < -1
20. x ≥ 2
21.
22.
23. Table finished:
   -3, 7; (-3, 7)
   -2, 6; (-2, 6)
   -1, 5; (-1, 5)
   0, 4; (0, 4)
24. Table finished:
   -4, -8; (-4, -8)
   -2, -4; (-2, -4)
   0, 0; (0, 0)
   2, 4; (2, 4)
   1, 3; (1, 3)
   2, 2 (2, 2)
   4, 8; (4, 8)
   6, 12; (6, 12)
25. b
26. d

Part Four: Geometry

1. 5,000 m²; use the formula for area: multiply 100 m by 50 m
2. 1,250 m²; take $\frac{1}{8}$ (or $\frac{1}{4}$) of the entire area
3. 1,250 m²; take $\frac{2}{8}$ (or $\frac{1}{4}$) of the entire area
4. 1,875 m²; take $\frac{3}{8}$ of the entire area
5. 625 m²; take $\frac{1}{8}$ of entire area
6. 120 m
7. 420 ft²
8. 2,640 cm²
9. 55 cm
10. 2,520 ft³
11. 5 units
12. 16 units
13. 17.5 units²
14. 13 units
15. (1, 6)
16. (-4, 8)
17. 20 units²
18. 7 units
19. 10 cm
20. 2.2
21. rectangular prism
22. 220 in²

Part Five: Statistics Part Five: Statistics and Probability

1. a, c, d, e
2. no
3. no
4. no
5. yes
6. 17
7. 15
8. 16
9. Answers will vary; the argument
   could be made for 15 (the median) because it is closer to half the data items (11, 12, 13, 14)
10. 6
11. 29 (11-40)
12. 3.5 (12.5-16)
13. interquartile range; explanations will vary— with the outlier (40) removed, the interquartile range shows the smaller variation
   among the rest of the data
14. 3
15. concussions
16. about 205 (following the trend of an increase from 85-145 from Jan to Feb)
17. about 160 (about 30-190)
18. A. Check line plot for the following values:
   0-11
   1-10
   2-8
   3-10
   4-8
   5-6
   6-4
   7-3
   8-5
   9-2
   10-4
   11-0
   12-2
   13-1
   14-0
   15-1
   16-0
   B. Observations will vary. Make sure observations are valid. Students may observe that the greatest frequency is in the 0 to 4 range.

ACTIVITIES ANSWER KEY

Ratios and Proportional Relationships (pages 18-34)

pages 18-19

1. 5 to 12
2. 6 to 5 (or $\frac{6}{5}$ or 6:5)
3. 6 to 24 (or $\frac{6}{24}$ or 6:24)
4. 1 to 4 (or $\frac{1}{4}$ or 1:4)
5. $\frac{2}{1}$ (or 2 to 1 or 2:1)
6. 6 to 1 (or $\frac{6}{1}$ or 6:1)
7. 11 to 1 (or $\frac{11}{1}$ or 11:1)
8. $\frac{1}{7}$
9. $\frac{1}{4}$
10. $\frac{1}{5}$
11. 1 to 15
12. 6:1
13. b
14. e
15. d

page 20

1. $3.20
2. 15
3. 9
4. 2,020
5. 7
6. 4
7. 67

page 21

1. c
2. a
3. d
4. b
5. d
6. b
7. a
8. c

page 22

1. Completed table pairs across: $\frac{5}{12}$, $\frac{10}{24}$, $\frac{15}{36}$, $\frac{20}{48}$, $\frac{25}{60}$, $\frac{30}{72}$ Answer: 30
2. Completed table pairs across: $\frac{18}{11}$, $\frac{36}{22}$, $\frac{54}{33}$, $\frac{72}{44}$, $\frac{90}{55}$, $\frac{108}{66}$; Answer: 66
3. Completed table pairs across: $\frac{4}{9}$, $\frac{8}{18}$, $\frac{12}{27}$, $\frac{16}{36}$, $\frac{20}{45}$, $\frac{24}{54}$ Answer: 4
4. Completed table pairs across: $\frac{1.5}{3}$, $\frac{3}{2}$, $\frac{6}{4}$, $\frac{9}{6}$; $\frac{12}{8}$, $\frac{15}{10}$, $\frac{18}{12}$, $\frac{24}{16}$ Answer: 1.5 hours

page 23

Students may set up tables differently. Check tables to see that they correctly display equivalent ratios, leading to a correct answer.

1. Answer 42

2. Roxanne ($\frac{1}{5}$ is higher than $\frac{1}{6}$)
3. Liam

pages 24-25

1. Completed table pairs across: $\frac{0}{0}$, $\frac{3}{2}$, $\frac{6}{4}$, $\frac{9}{6}$, $\frac{12}{8}$, $\frac{15}{10}$ Answer: 12
2. B
3. D
4. A
5. C
6. Look for line E to be drawn through points (8, 4) and (16, 8)

pages 26-27

1. a. 808 km; b. 202 km/hr
2. a. Train A; 80 mi
3. 150 km/hr
4. 300
5. a. 70 mph; b. 75 mph; c. no
6. a. 82 mph; b. 1,722 miles
7. a. the train; b. yes
8. Up the mountain is 45 mph; down is 54 mph; difference is 9 mph
9. a. 47; b. 16

page 28

1. 40 cents
2. $1.52
3. 93 cents
4. $1.60
5. 65 cents
6. $6.50
7. 90 cents
8. $3.50
9. $14.50
10. chocolate truffles

page 29

Total score: 350
1. 16.7%
2. 50%
3. 16.7%
4. 42.9%
5. 75
6. 100
7. 25
8. 451
9. 30%
10. 192
11. 275%
12. 130
13. 300,000
14. 80

page 30

1. yes
2. 17,600
3. 61.8%
4. 75%
5. 1,017
6. 6,840,000
7. 3.6%

page 31

1. 400,000
2. 130,000
3. 24,640
4. 104,000
5. 58%
6. 104,125
7. 15%
8. 68%
9. 78,500
10. 83,600

page 32

Answers may vary somewhat.
Fred: $36.67 (Subt. $30.30, tip $4.55, tax $1.82)
Red: $32.19 (Subt. $26.60, tip $3.99, tax $1.60)
Tad: $39.20 (Subt. $32.40, tip $4.86, tax $1.94)
Brad: $17.42 (Subt. $14.40, tip $2.16, tax $0.86)
Chad: $40.54 (Subt. $33.50, tip $5.03, tax $2.01)

pages 33-34

1. 0.18 m
2. 33,180 ft
3. 68,000 g
4. 87 oz
5. 1,700 ml
6. 1,520
7. 5,000 lb
8. no (50,000 g)
9. no (4 min, 23 sec)
10. yes
11. no (1.08 l)
12. no (364 ft)
13. b
14. b
15. a
16. c
17. 11.373 l
18. 2 hr, 55 min
19. 340.2
20. Joe's
21. 554 yd, 2 ft
22. Greg

The Number System (pages 36-60)

pages 36-37

1. Solution is 3. Diagram should show boxes drawn around 3 groups of $\frac{2}{8}$.
2. Solution is 4. Diagram should show boxes drawn around 4 groups of $\frac{3}{8}$.
3. Solution is 3. Diagram should show boxes drawn around 3 groups of $\frac{3}{4}$.
4. Solution is 6. Diagram should show 1 whole and $\frac{1}{3}$ of a second whole shaded, with lines dividing both wholes into ninths. Six groups of $\frac{2}{9}$ should be delineated with boxes.
5. Solution is 6. Diagram should show $\frac{4}{5}$ of a whole shaded with lines dividing the whole into 15ths. Six groups of $\frac{2}{15}$ should be delineated with boxes.
6. Solution is 4. Diagram should show $\frac{6}{7}$ of a whole shaded, with lines dividing the whole into 14ths. Four groups of $\frac{3}{14}$ should be delineated with boxes.
7. Problems will vary. Check to see that the problem fits the equation (and its solution) and that it is a logical division problem.

page 38

1. 324
2. 303
3. 21
4. 46
5. 40
6. 17
7. 120
8. 540 cm
9. 3,650
10. 35

page 39

1. 322
2. 45
3. 35
4. 555
5. 823
6. 70

page 40

Dominic	Gianna
1. 0.24	1. yes
2. 122	2. 116
3. yes	3. 6.7
4. 11	4. 33
5. 6.8	5. 9.2

Common Core Reinforcement Activities — 6th Grade Math

page 41
1. 5.414 m/s
2. 6.003 m/s
3. 36.23 s
4. 14.58 s
5. 80.02 kg
6. 24.47 s
7. 11,025 m

page 42
A. 1, 2, 4, 8, 16
B. 4, 8, 12, 16, 20
C. 1, 5, or 25
D. 5, 10, 15, 20, 25
E. 1, 2, 3, 6
F. Answers will vary. Check for accuracy. (Could be 35, 70, 105 . . .)
G. 1, 2, 4, 11, 22, 44
H. 1, 2, 3, 6, 9, 18
I. Answers will vary. Check for accuracy. (Could be 6, 12, 18, 24, 30 . . .)
J. Answers will vary. Check for accuracy. (Could be 24, 48, 72, 96 . . .)
K. 1, 2, 3, 4, 6, 8, 12, 16, 24, 48
L. 6
M. 8
N. 20
O. 12
P. 36
Q. 16
R. Explanations will vary. Check for accuracy. LCM is 210.
S. Answers will vary. Check for accuracy. (Could be 18, 36, 54, . . .)

page 43
1. GCF; four sets (9 towels and 7 bottles in each)
2. LCM; Locker #24
3. LCM; 18
4. LCM; 2 pizzas and 3 sets of drinks
5. GCF; six boxes (2 white and 7 milk in each)
6. GCF; 3 ft; 8 pieces
7. LCM; 5 packages rolls, 4 packages hot dogs (LCM is 40)

page 44
1. 9(11 + 6) = 153
2. 9(5 + 10) = 135
3. 7(9 + 12) = 147
4. 36(4 + 1) = 180
5. 11(7 + 2) = 99
6. 3(32 + 7) = 117
7. 8(2 + 7) = 72
8. 6(15 + 8) = 138
9. 24(1 + 3) = 96
10. 21(1 + 4) = 105

page 45
1. -12 °C
2. 2 °C
3. -18 °C
4. -14 °C
5. no
6. freezing point of water
7. 15
8. - 4
9. b
10. -20

page 46
1. 14   5. -65   9. -46
2. -36.5   6. -38   10. 23
3. -40   7. 67   11. -110
4. 87   8. -75

page 47
1. Shane
2. Brie and Anton
3. -12
4. 16.6 m
5. -8
6. 8
7. They are opposites. They are 16 units apart.
8. 4
9. -4
10. Check drawings for correct location at -3.5.

page 48
1. (2, 6)
2. D
3. IV
4. B
5. (9, -4)
6. Check for correct location of ant P at (-5, 3).
7. (-7, 0)
8. (8, -1)
9. M
10. III
11. E
12. (3, -5)
13. Check for correct location of ant Q at (0, -6).
14. C

page 49
CHECK FOR REFLECTIONS, NOT SLIDES
1. Check for new locations: A_1 (0, 3); B_1 (0, 0); C_1 (4, 0); D_1 (4, 3)
2. Check for new locations: W_1 (6, 4); X_1 (6, 6); Y_1 (1, 6); Z_1 (1, 4)
3. (-5, 4) across the x-axis and (5, -4) across the y-axis
4. (0, -5)
5. Check for new locations: J_1 (2, 6); K_1 (2.5, 3) L_1 (4.5, 3); M_1 (5, 6)
6. Check for new locations: P_1 (-1, 2); Q_1 (-1, -3); R_1 (-4, -3)
7. (-8, 5)

page 50
1. -3
2. B
3. -0.5 (or $-\frac{1}{2}$)
4. 2.5 (or $2\frac{1}{2}$)
5. Check for a parachute drawn at -5.5 (labeled M).
6. 2.8 or $2\frac{4}{5}$
7. S
8. W
9. -0.4 or $-\frac{2}{5}$
10. Check for a parachute drawn at -1.6 ($-1\frac{3}{5}$), labeled Z.

page 51
Check to see that points are plotted correctly, yielding an abominable snowman figure that looks like this:

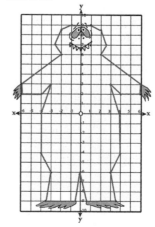

page 52
1. 350 > 0
2. 0 < 350
3. -500 < 0
4. 350 > -500
5. -500 < 350
6. 0 > -500

page 53
1. -2 < 22 (or 22 > -2)
2. -14 °C < 22 °C (or 22 °C > -14 °C)
3. -14 °C < -6 °C (or 6 °C > -14 °C)
4. -$60 < $80 (or $80 > -$60)
5. -$35 is to the left of $48 dollars on a number line.
6. Zero is to the right of -55, which is to the right of -59 on a number line.
7. 5 degrees is above -15 degrees on the Celsius thermometer.
8. -18 is to the left of -8 on a number line
9. 6.8 is to the right of -20.5 on a number line.

page 54
1. yes
2. -$155; $150; $150.55
3. c
4. $-3\frac{1}{4}$; $-\frac{7}{9}$; 0.9
5. c
6. $-\frac{20}{30}$; -0.5; $\frac{1}{5}$
7. a
8. -8.05; 0.85; $8\frac{3}{4}$

page 55
1. a loss of twenty-two and one-half yards on the play
2. team has a debt of $250
3. temperature is 5 degrees F below zero
4. bus drove 20 kilometers per hour below the speed limit
5. $\frac{3}{4}$
6. $89.75
7. 0.76
8. $\frac{20}{27}$
9. 65.4
10. 37
11. 0
12. 35
13. 35.5

14. no
15. yes
16. two (8.8 and -8.8)

page 56
1. $900
2. $950
3. a. -$52; b. $52
4. T
5. F
6. T
7. F

page 57

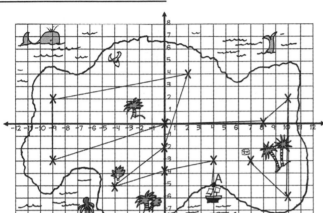

1. no
2. whale

pages 58-59
1. c
2. (4, -5)
3. (-4, 0)
4. baseball
5.-12. Check student drawings for accuracy of locations. #11, the helmet, should be drawn on the dresser.
13. 11 feet
14. 10 feet
15. 7 feet
16. 14 feet
17. yes
18. Check to see that line connects the hockey puck at (4, -5) to (4, 7).

page 60
1. II
2. IV
3. A
4. (7, 6)
5. (3, -7)
6. R (2, 6); S (-6, 0); T (2, 0)
7. 13 units

8. 12 units
9. 9 units
10. 28 units

Expressions and Equations (pages 62-88)

page 62
1. Matt
2. Matt
3. Toni
4. 6^9
5. $(3 + 15)^2$
6. 5^4
7. -3^5
8. 64,000,000
9. $\frac{16}{256}$ (or $\frac{1}{16}$)
10. 0.015625
11. -10,000,000,000
12. $\frac{3}{5}$
13. $27\frac{1}{9}$
14. 1

page 63
1. Chad: 125 min; Basha: 27 min; Toni: 16 min; Zoey: 8 min; Matt: 4 min; Total: 180 min (or 3 hr)
2. the difference between four times a number and two times that same number squared
3. a number multiplied by itself eight times
4. (the sum of negative six and three) multiplied by itself three times
5. $\frac{10^6}{5}$ (or $10^6 \div 5$)
6. $(-1\frac{1}{2})^3$
7. $(18 + 3)^2$
8. 200

9. $27n^3 + 8$
10. $-\frac{8}{125}$
11. 1
12. 1,000,000
13. 36
14. -32
15. -216
16. $7a^6$

page 64
Introductory question:
s = 2t – 3

1. c	3. c	5. a	7. b
2. a	4. b	6. b	8. c

page 65
1. m + 3
2. 15r – 7j
3. 4p – 2n
4. 12t – 4t
5. 8c – 5
6. 2(2b + 6j)
7. 3(2s – 5f)
8. 10h + s + 2p
9. 2a < 3p
10. 5(b + a)
11. ($\frac{1}{2}$r + $\frac{1}{4}$t)
12. 10(b + f) > 5a

page 66
1. 2 (z, x)
2. 2 (b, a)
3. 2 (k, m)
4. 4 (p, q, r, s)
5. L
6. U
7. U
8. U
9. 2
10. 4
11. 4
12. 1
13. $7z$, $\frac{18m}{2}$, $\frac{1}{2}b$, z
14. 7z and z
15. $\frac{18}{2}$
16. $\frac{1}{2}$

page 67
1. B, C, D, F, H, I, K, L
2. B
3. A, B, C, D, F, G, J, K, L
4. A
5. D
6. L
7. B, C, E, G, J, K
8. B
9. A, E, G, J
10. C, F, J

page 68
Yes, the expression at the beginning of the page is true.
1. 3w + 2p; $498
2. 4(4f + s); $1,008
3. 2c + 10; $74
4. 3b – 3; $477
5. f < 2t; $18 < $400
6. 3(p + b); $1,200
7. $\frac{5w}{2}$; $15
8. (c + 2w + f) < 100; $62 < $100

page 69
1. 52 oz
2. 64 g
3. 216,000 cm^3
4. 27 ft^2
5. 30
6. 121
7. 6 m^2
8. 2.6 hr
9. 30.6 l (liters)
10. 16 yd
11. -4
12. 18
13. -120

page 70
1. 8a
2. 7x – 6
3. 8k
4. 6c + 6
5. 7n
6. 4x+ 2 + y + 0.6
   Simplified:
   4x + y + 2.6 = 6.1 km
7. z+ 2x + y + z
   Simplified:
   2z + 2x + y = 4.1 km
8. 2x + y + z + z + y + 0.6 + 4x + 2 + 2.5y + 2x + 0.3 + y + x
   Simplified: 9x + 5.5y + 2z + 2.9 = 17.25 km

page 71
1. identity
2. associative
3. commutative
4. opposites
5. distributive
6. distributive
7. 20p + 10q
8. 3b^2 – 15b
9. c + d
10. 21g – 180
11. 76n
12. 40c^2
13. 8x^2 – 5x + 2
14. 5

page 72
1. c
2. c
3. a
4. b
5. 4
6. 3y + 20 = 35
7. 2x + z^2 – z = 4
8. b^2 + by – n = 11

Common Core Reinforcement Activities — 6th Grade Math

page 73

Pairs of equivalent expressions, in no particular order:

$2(6 + k)$ and $2k + 12$

$5y^2 + 3xy + y^2 - 8xy$ and $6y^2 - 5xy$

$4b(b^2 + 5)$ and $4b^3 + 20b$

$(j)(j)(j)$ and j^3

$7(2 - x)$ and $14 - 7x$

$x(x + 12)$ and $x^2 + 12x$

$10(x + 3) + x$ and $11x + 30$

$(ab)(3ab)$ and $3a^2b^2$

page 74

1. Color the following boxes and join them in this order: A, D, C, E, F, G, I, L, N, M, O.

page 75

A. yes	I. no
B. yes	J. no
C. yes	K. no
D. yes	L. yes
E. no	M. no
F. no	N. no
G. yes	O. yes
H. no	P. no

page 76

Equations may vary. Check to see that each equation is one that can actually solve the problem.

1. $c = \frac{32}{2}$; $c = 16$
2. $2l = 27 + 9$; $l = 18$
3. $4t = 16.4$; $t = 4.1$ kg
4. $67 + f = 86$; $f = 19$
5. $n = \frac{72}{3}$; $n = 24$ kg
6. $3t = (95 - 5)$; 30 °F

page 77

1. c; $x = 26$
2. b; Matt ate fewer than 9.
3. c; $d = 3$
4. a; $m = 3$
5. b; $m = 6$
6. Equations may vary. Check to see that the equation is one that can actually solve the problem. $\frac{13.50}{b} = 1.50$; $b = 9$

page 78

Equations may vary. Check to see that each equation is one that can actually solve the problem.

1. $21 - t = 14$; $t = 7$ min
2. $w = 100 - 41$; $w = 59$ lb
3. $d = \frac{0.9}{2} - 0.06$; $d = 0.39$ km
4. $r = 2(3 + 6)$; $r = 18$
5. $50 - m = 33$; $m = 17$ min
6. $18 = 3b$; $b = 6$
7. $100 + 70 + p = 208$; $p = 38$ lb

page 79

1. $y = 18.08$
2. $d = 30$
3. $n = 2$
4. $z = 4$
5. $k = 6.5$
6. $p = 12$
7. $g = 17$
8. $b = 33$
9. $3,500t = 22,750$; $t = 6.5$ sec
10. $115 + s = 304$; $s = 189$

page 80

The top solution is correct.

1. C
2. C
3. C
4. $q = 5,000$
5. $k = 36$
6. $d = 18.4$
7. C
8. C
9. C
10. C
11. $w = 1.8$ l (liters)
12. C
13. $t = 3.5$ hr

page 81

Equations may vary. Check to see that each equation is one that can actually solve the problem.

1. $12 - p = 5\frac{1}{2}$; $p = 6\frac{1}{2}$
2. $p = 7\frac{1}{2} - 3$; $p = 4\frac{1}{2}$
3. $b = (\frac{16}{2}) - 3$; $b = 5$
4. $2(32) - w = 7$; $w = 57$ oz
5. $b + 14 = 27$; $b = 13$
6. $3b = 18$; $b = 6$
7. $5s = 2,990$; $s = 598$ g

page 82

Question in introduction: $x = 0.25$ inches

ACROSS

A. 46	T. 49
E. 27	U. 308
G. 2,111	V. 111
H. 7,000	X. 63
I. 64	Y. 4,008
J. 29	Z. 15
L. 12	BB. 375
M. 925	EE. 65
P. 55,005	FF. 16
R. 99	GG. 64
S. 21	

DOWN

B. 600	O. 59
C. 81	Q. 518
D. 316	T. 4,116
F. 72	U. 333
G. 202	V. 1,006
H. 749	W. 189
K. 9,520	AA. 55
L. 15,010	CC. 71
N. 299	DD. 56

page 83

1. 6, 4
2. -1
3. -6, -2, 7
4. -5, 3, -2
5. 6, 0
6. 11
7. -4, 3, -6
8. 3, -2, 0
9. 7, 16, 20, -5
10. -1, -4, -6
11. $x + 10 > 18$
12. $3x + 6 \leq 2$

page 84

1. $x < 2$
2. $x > -2$
3. $x \geq -1$
4. $x \leq 3$
5.-8. Check student graphs:
5. closed circle at -1, arrow extending left
6. closed circle at -3, arrow extending right
7. open circle at -4, arrow extending right
8. open circle at 5, arrow extending left

page 85

Completed tables read:

A.

12	60	(12, 60)
10	50	(10, 50)
8	40	(8, 40)
6	30	(6, 30)
4	20	(4, 20)
2	10	(2, 10)

B.

-3	2	(-3, 2)
-1	4	(-1, 4)
0	5	(0, 5)
1	6	(1, 6)
2	7	(2, 7)
3	8	(3, 8)

C.

4	2	(4, 2)
-2	-1	(-2, -1)
0	0	(0, 0)
2	1	(2, 1)
4	2	(4, 2)
6	3	(6, 3)

D.

-8	-2	(-8, -2)
-5	-1	(-5, -1)
-2	0	(-2, 0)
1	1	(1, 1)
4	2	(4, 2)
7	3	(7, 3)

E.

-5	-15	(-5, -15)
-3	-9	(-3, -9)
-1	-3	(-1, -3)
0	0	(0, 0)
2	6	(2, 6)
5	15	(5, 15)

pages 86-87

In the introductory graph, the hook in Quadrant I at (-4, -2) is attached to Mike's line. Check to see that any lines drawn on graphs pass through accurately plotted points.

Completed tables or pairs read:

A. Hook in Quadrant III at (-4, -4)

-4	-4	(-4, -4)
-3	2	(-3, 2)
-2	0	(-2, 0)
-1	2	(-1, 2)
0	4	(0, 4)
1	6	(1, 6)

B. Hook in Quadrant IV at (4, -4)

-3	3	(-3, 3)
-2	2	(-2, 2)
1	-1	(1, -1)
2	-2	(2, -2)
3	-3	(3, -3)
4	-4	(4, -4)

C.
(-2, -4); (0, 0); (1, 2); (2, 4)

D.
(-1, 3); (0, 1); (1, -1); (2, -3)

E.
(-4, 1); (-3, 2); (-2, 3); (-1, 4)

F.
Equation c matches the graph.

page 88
1. 7
2. 11
Completed tables or pairs read:

A.

2	12	(2, 12)
4	10	(4, 10)
5	9	(5, 9)
8	6	(8, 6)
10	4	(10, 4)
12	2	(12, 2)

B.

-5	-8	(-5, -8)
3	0	(3, 0)
0	-3	(0, -3)
-2	-5	(-2, -5)
5	2	(5, 2)
-1	-4	(-1, -4)

C.

-3	12	(-3, 12)
2	-8	(2, -8)
-1	4	(-1, 4)
4	-16	(4, -16)
-5	20	(-5, 20)
7	-28	(7, -28)

D.

-5	13	(-5, 13)
-3	9	(-3, 9)
-1	5	(-1, 5)
0	3	(0, 3)
3	-3	(3, -3)
6	-9	(6, -9)

E.

0	-3	(0, -3)
4	-1	(4, -1)
6	0	(6, 0)
10	2	(10, 2)
14	4	(14, 4)
16	5	(16, 5)

Geometry (pages 90-106)

page 90
1. 5,000 yd^2
2. 1,250 yd^2
3. 625 yd^2
4. 1,250 yd^2
5. 3,125 yd^2
6. 1,875 yd^2

page 91
1. 625 m^2
2. 200 m^2
3. 200 m^2
4. 425 m^2

5. 100 m^2
6. 112.5 m^2

pages 92-93
1. 121 m^2
2. 1,456 ft^2
3. 325 m^2
4. 125 m^2
5. 1,848,750 cm^2
6. 9.6 ft^2
7. 46.4 ft^2
8. 480 m^2
9. 285 m^2
10. yes
11. 2,900 m^2
12. 72 m^2
13. Color rectangle in lower part of figure.
14. b

page 94
1. 900 m^2
2. 24 ft^2
3. 12 m
4. 351 ft^2
5. 1,200 ft^2
6. 1.04 m^2
7. 250 m^2

page 95
Answers will vary depending on the student's box measurements and the size of the cubic unit chosen. Ask students to show their problem-solving process.

page 96
1. V = 1,522.5 cm^3
2. h = 14.5 cm
3. V = 3,875 cm^3
4. w = 8 cm
5. w = 10 cm
6. V = 3,537.5 cm^3
7. h = 9 cm
A. Maya and Val (1,522.5 cm^3 and 1,530 cm^3)
B. Joe

page 97
1. yes
2. 200
3. 1,701,000
4. 9,576
5. 0.5 m
6. Answers may vary. One way to do this is: 5 rows of 6 boxes across the box. 4 stacks high.

pages 98-99
1. D
2. E
3. H
4. C
5. B
6. A
7. F
8. G

pages 100-101
1. triangle
2. There are several options. Here are two possibilities: points G, H, I, and (8.5, -8) or points DFE, and (-4. -5)
3. 6.5 m
4. (4, -3) or (-6, 3)
5. (9, -8)
6. (6, -7)
7. right triangle
8. (-9, 3)
9. a. 6-sided polygon (two rectangles perpendicular to each other)
   b. 12 m
   c. 13m^2

pages 102-103
1. Check to see that skateboard silhouettes are drawn at each given location.
2. 2.7 km
3. 9.6 km^2
4. Check drawings for points at given locations.
5. 4.5 km^2
6. (-4, 5)
7. 6.3 km (if he follows just one vertical and one horizontal line on the most direct path)
8. 21 km
9. triangle; check drawings for points at given locations.

page 104
1. 9 edges, 5 faces, 2 bases, 6 vertices
2. 12 edges. 6 faces, 2 bases, 8 vertices
3. 12 edges. 6 faces, 2 bases, 8 vertices
4. b

5. 24 cm^2
6. b

page 105
Observe students as they complete the 1-7 instructions.
3. 9
4. 6
6. Surface area will vary depending on size of image after copying. Check to see that they have measured and calculated the surface area accurately.

page 106
1. 31
2. 121.2 ft^2
3. 12.6 m^2
4. 1,200 ft^2
5. 3.84 m^2
6. 696 cm^2

Statistics and Probability (pages 108-126)

page 108

1. b, d	4. yes
2. a, d	5. no
3. yes	

page 109
1. no; there is no variability in the answer
2. yes
3. no
4. no; there is no variability in the answer
5. yes; there is variability in the answer
6. no; there is no variability in the answer

page 110
A. Check student line plots for the following numbers of X's:

0—0	6—7	12—4
1—0	7—8	13—4
2—1	8—7	14—0
3—2	9—8	15—1
4—3	10—	16—1
5—7	11—11	

B. 76 skiers; Description of the data will vary, but it should include reference to the bell-shaped curve, cluster of most X's between 5 and 11, with greatest frequencies at 10 and 11.

page 111
1. 10, 64, 66, 69, 81, 98, 100, 136, 255
2. 81
3. 245
4. 71
5. 174
6. Observations about the data will vary. Accept answers with reasonable assessments and conclusions.

page 112
1. 14 (3-17)
2. 11
3. 11
4. 16
5. range
6. mean, median
7. range 12 (40-52); median: 44; mean: 45; mode: 41
8. range 9 (0-9); median: 4; mean: 4; mode: 2

page 113
1. 16 (4-20)
2. 10.4
3. 10
4. 10
5. range: 7 (14-21); mean: 17
6. 7 hours
7. above
8. 1.2 kg

page 114
1-9. Check to see that points are plotted to match the data in the problems.
10. Data descriptions will vary. Students may observe that he began and ended the 11 months with "easier" climbs and peaked mid-year with higher climbs.

page 115
A. Check student graphs to see that data is properly plotted.

B. Data descriptions will vary. Students may observe that Trash Dashers and Rubbish Kings started strong and had shorter distances over the six weeks, with a brief rally each, while the Bin Brigade showed the greatest gains over the time period.

page 116
1. 12
2. 4
3. 4 and 7
4. 0
5. c

page 117
A. Check to see that the following numbers of X's have been placed above these numbers:

3—1	16—7
5—1	17—6
6—1	18—2
7—2	20—2
8—2	21—2
9—1	22—2
10—1	28—1
13—4	29—1
14—6	31—1
15—5	

B. 48
C. 13 to 17 cm
D. Answers will vary. Students may observe few bubbles in the 3- to 12-cm size, and few over 17 cm, with most falling from 13- to 17-cm in size.

page 118
1. Rhonda and Roxy
2. Rex and Ryan
3. Rex
4. Reba and Ryan
5. Roxy
6. Roxy
7. Reba and Rhonda
8. b

page 119
A. Check to see that data have been accurately displayed.
B. Answers will vary. Students may observe

that broken legs and head injuries constitute the lowest numbers of injuries.

page 120
1. 35-39
2. 60-64, 65-69, 70+
3. about 73
4. 45-49, 55-59, 60-64, 65-69, 70+
5. 40-49 (40-44 and 45-49)
6. 15-19
7. 35-39 and 40-44
8. Answers will vary. Students might observe that most competitors fall between age 10 and 44 or that the largest groups are in the 15-34 range. They may observe that there is a respectable number of older competitors but that over 44 ranges are the smallest numbers.

page 121
Check to see that data have been accurately displayed: 0-499—58; 500-999—73; 1,000-1,499—55; 1,500-1,999—61; 2,000-2,499—38; 2,500 and over—20.

page 122
1. unusual items eaten or swallowed
2. individual items
3. 8
4. sausages
5. Answers will vary. Students might conclude that it is easier to eat pickled onions fast than it is to eat the other items.
6. Answers will vary.

page 123
1. weight of snowballs
2. pounds
3. 6 days
4. number of pounds of snowballs increased each day
5. no
6. yes
7. no

8. no
9. no

pages 124-125
1. 100
2. 100
3. about 23.3 m
4. about 1.3
5. 78 to 127 or 49 m
6. 2,045
7. c
8. c
9. 355 to 450 or 95 hr
10. 392.9
11. 3
12. 15
13. Answers will vary. The mode is the lowest number of hours ridden and does not reflect the center well. The mean and median are better indications of central tendency for this data.

page 126
1. median—4 of the 7 data items are close to the median
2. 31 (10-41)
3. 29
4. 4
5. 5.6
6. 4
7. 3
8. median; the 19 is so much greater than the other numbers that it skews the mean to be unrepresentative of the center for the other numbers
9. 18 (1-19)
10. 3
11. interquartile range; the 19 is so much greater than the other numbers that it skews the range to be unrepresentative of the majority of the data